GOLD
Pupil's Book

Nigel Heslop David Brodie James Williams
George Snape Marguerite Hall

Hodder & Stoughton
A MEMBER OF THE HODDER HEADLINE GROUP

Photo acknowledgements

The publishers would like to thank the following individuals, institutions and companies for permission to reproduce photographs in this book. Every effort has been made to trace ownership of copyright. The publishers would be happy to make arrangements with any copyright holder whom it has not been possible to contact:

Action Plus (4 left, 39 both, 40 left, 49); Andrew Lambert (17, 21 all, 27 right, 56 top, 57 top & bottom, 92 all except olivine & diamond, 105, 106 right, 108 bottom); Army (117 right); Associated Press (54 left, 102 top right, 114); British Antarctic Survey (32 both); Bruce Coleman Ltd (117 both left, 119, 149); Corbis (25, 37 left, 57 middle, 60, 65, 79 top and middle left, 104, 113, 122, 125b, d, e, 131, 136, 148); Culver Pictures Inc (132); Davant Products Ltd (36); GSF Picture Library (95 right, 128 left three and bottom right, 135 both); Nigel Heslop (56 bottom); Hodder & Stoughton (54 top right, 123 bottom); ISG Thermal Systems Ltd (35); Life File (1 both, 2 both, 3 top two, 4 right, 8, 9 all, 18 Figures 1 & 4–7, 20 top, 27 left, 28 both, 36 left, 40 right, 41, 54 bottom right, 78 bottom left, 89, 90 all, 91 top two, 95 both left, 97, 101, 102 both left, 106 left, 108, 122 top & bottom, 123 top, 125a & c, 128 top right, 131 left); Mary Evans Picture Library (16 top right, 79 middle right); Moviestore (63, 139); Natural History Museum (129 bottom); Omicron (14); Oxford Scientific Films (116 both); Redferns (143, 144 both); Ronald Grant Archive (110); Science Photo Library (10, 44 right, 47 right, 67, 80, 85, 86, 91 bottom left, 97, 129 top, 137)/Adam Hart-Davis (46)/Alfred Pasieka (18 Figure 8)/Biophoto Associates (3 bottom two)/Bruce Iverson (34)/BSIP DR LR (147 top)/BSIP Laurent (42 bottom right)/Charles D Winters (23, 92 second from top)/Conor Caffrey (48 right)/Damien Lovegrove (48 left)/David Parker (18 Figure 3, 111)/ Dr P Marazzi (78 right)/Eye of Science (76a, 84 left)/George Post (102 bottom right)/John Bavosi (42 top right)/John Radcliffe Hospital (44 left)/Juergen Berger (76b)/Martin Bond (18 Figure 2)/Matt Meadows, Peter Arnold Inc. (77)/Maximilian Stock Ltd (37 right)/Paul Shambroom (16 bottom right)/Phil Jude (6)/Robert Knowles (96)/Rosenfeld Images Ltd (78 top left)/Sheila Terry (84 right)/Simon Fraser, Mauna Loa Observatory (31)/Sinclair Stammers (92 second from bottom)/ St Mary's Hospital Medical School (79 bottom)/Tek Image (20 bottom right)/Tony Craddock (98); The Wellcome Trust (147 bottom)

Orders: please contact Bookpoint Ltd, 130 Milton Park, Abingdon, Oxon OX14 4SB. Telephone: (44) 01235 827720. Fax: (44) 01235 400454. Lines are open from 9.00–6.00, Monday to Saturday, with a 24 hour message answering service.
You can also order through our website www.hodderheadline.co.uk

British Library Cataloguing in Publication Data

A catalogue record for this title is available from the British Library

ISBN 0 340 80439 4

First published 2002

Impression number   10 9 8 7 6 5 4
Year   2008 2007 2006 2005 2004 2003

Copyright © 2002 Nigel Heslop, James Williams, George Snape, Marguerite Hall, David Brodie

Cover photo from Science Photo Library.

Typeset by Fakenham Photosetting.

Printed in Italy for Hodder & Stoughton Educational, a division of Hodder Headline, 338 Euston Road, London NW1 3BH.

Contents

Preface

Hodder Science is a collection of resources designed to match exactly the QCA exemplar Scheme of Work for KS3. The core material of the series is suitable for the more able two-thirds of pupils. The scheme has successfully moved away from the minimalist approach of the past decade, is pupil-friendly and easy to read.

Hodder Science Gold has been written to extend the range of the *Hodder Science* series, specifically catering for the lower 30–35% of the ability range. These books will progressively target levels 2 to 4/5 of the National Curriculum.

Hodder Science Gold takes a new attitude to producing books for the lower attainer. It does far more than just present the same learning material at a slightly lower reading age. Marguerite Hall, a well-known learning methods consultant, has lent her expertise to increase the friendliness of the text and the accessibility of the way the ideas are presented. We have taken an integrated approach to producing material aimed at low attainers for the 21st Century.

- Key words boxes highlight and define target vocabulary on the spread where the terms are first used.
- Concepts are introduced at a level and rate more suitable for slower learners.
- Progression, through the concepts and models used, is tailored to the needs of a slower learner.
- There is no compromise on essential learning vocabulary, but peripheral vocabulary is kept to a simple reading level.
- Reading level concentrates on good sentence structure to make the flow of reading easier.
- Sometimes a few more simple words are used to explain a difficult concept rather than rigidly cutting word count.
- Generally word count per page is one half to two thirds of the parallel *Hodder Science* books.
- The number and style of questions has been altered to enable slower pupils to keep pace.
- Essential summary tasks contain a high level of prompt to ensure accuracy and success.
- To aid parallel use of the books, the spread by spread structure exactly mirrors the higher level books.
- To avoid stigmatisation of the lower attainer, many illustrations are the same and the book colour is the same. The gold trim signifies that these books are special.

Nigel Heslop 2002

CHAPTER 1

Food and digestion

In Great Britain we spend nearly £3 billion a year on fast food. We eat lots of burgers, pizzas and fried chicken! Most of us love 'junk food'. Is it really that bad for us? If we're not eating properly, what should we be eating? What does our body do with the food that we eat?

This chapter will look at what we eat and what we should eat. And we will look at how our body breaks down and uses what is in our food to keep us healthy and provide us with energy.

Questions

1 Look at the two photos on this page and sort the food into the following groups
   ★ Group 1 – Energy-giving foods
   ★ Group 2 – Foods to help you grow
   ★ Group 3 – Healthy food
   ★ Group 4 – Unhealthy foods

2 Athletes and sportsmen eat large amounts of food but never get fat. Why do you think this is?

3 Write down everything that you have eaten and drunk in the past two days. Do you think your diet is healthy or not?

4 Explain your answer to Question 3.

You are what you eat!

balanced diet   Eating the right amounts of each of the seven food types

carbohydrate   Food type, for energy

digestive system   The parts of the body that break down the food we eat (see page 7)

protein   Food type, for growth and repair

Questions

1   Look at the table below. Which are the two food types that give us 90% of the energy we need?

2   Where might we get the other 10% of our energy needs from?

3   What do we mean when we say that to be healthy we must eat a balanced diet?

4   Make up a diet sheet for yourself or a friend that provides a balanced diet without being boring (you can include some 'junk' food provided it is not too much and not too often!)

We need food to grow, be healthy and have energy. The food we eat is broken down in our **digestive system**. The chemicals from the food are transported around the body by the bloodstream. The chemicals that make up our food can be grouped into seven types. Each of the seven types is needed to keep us healthy. A **balanced diet** contains the right amount of all seven types.

Food type	Common foods	Why we need them
Carbohydrates (chemicals made from carbon, hydrogen and oxygen)	Bread, potatoes, rice, pasta, jam, sweets, fruit  **Figure 1** Food with lots of carbohydrate.	These are energy-giving foods. Nearly half (50%) of your energy needs come from carbohydrates.
Proteins	Meat, fish, eggs, cheese, milk, bread  **Figure 2** Foods with lots of protein.	These are needed to grow muscle and to repair our bodies. Muscles are made of protein. Some proteins give us energy.

Food type	Common foods	Why we need them
Fats	Butter, cream, oils, meat, cheese, margarine	Up to 40% of the energy you need will come from fats. The body stores energy as fat.
Figure 3 Foods with lots of fat.		
Minerals	Cheese, milk (contain calcium)	Calcium is good for bones and teeth.
	Liver, eggs, bread (contain iron)	Iron is needed for making haemoglobin for the blood. Haemoglobin makes our blood red in colour. It allows our blood carry oxygen.
	Salt (contains sodium)	Too little sodium can give you muscle cramp.
Figure 4 Foods with lots of minerals.		
Vitamins	A – liver, butter, green vegetables	Vitamin A is needed for good eyesight, especially in the dark!
	B_1 – bread, milk, potatoes, meat, yeast	
	B_2 – cheese, milk, liver, eggs	If we don't eat enough Vitamin B_2 we can get mouth sores and dry skin.
	B_{12} – meat, milk, yeast	Not enough vitamin B_{12} can lead to anaemia (fewer red blood cells than normal).
	C – oranges, lemons, fruits, green vegetables, tomatoes	Not enough vitamin C can cause scurvy (bleeding gums and internal bleeding).
	D – eggs, margarine, cod liver oil	Vitamin D is needed for healthy bones. If you don't eat enough vitamin D, you can get rickets (the bones are soft and can be bent out of shape as you grow!)
Figure 5 One symptom of scurvy is swollen, bleeding gums. **Figure 6** Rickets affects the bones of growing children		
Roughage (also known as fibre)	Vegetables, bread, cereals	Fibre helps to keep the intestines working properly.
Water	Many drinks, juices, milk and foods contain water	Two-thirds of you is water. An adult needs to drink about 2.5 litres of water each day. Without any water, a human being will die very quickly.

Diets

Do children need to diet?

Lots of young people, girls and boys, go on a diet at some time. Very often dieting is not necessary.

Figure 1   Exercise is a good way of losing weight and staying healthy.

Figure 2   Children come in lots of different shapes and sizes.

Magazines and newspapers are full of **diets**. Some diets are sensible, others could be dangerous.

Most people think that the easiest way to lose weight is to go on a diet. This is not always the best way to do it. Scientists have shown that nine times out of ten, weight lost during dieting is put back on at a later date!

If you look at Figure 2 you will see children of many different shapes and sizes. Until your late teens your body is still growing. If you grow quickly it can make you appear to be overweight when you are not. Very few children are so overweight that they need to diet. If you are very overweight, doctors call this being **obese**. Being obese can affect your health.

Read the following story about children in Hong Kong:

Children in Hong Kong are being warned of a serious risk to their health – obesity

Hong Kong children have changed from eating healthy diets to living on fast food and high fat snacks.

During break time, secondary school pupils crowd round food stalls buying fried chicken wings, crisps and other fatty snacks. Children are taller and fatter in Hong Kong than they used to be.

Plump children

Dr Henrietta Ip, a doctor who treats children, says parents like their children to be plump. 'They don't see overweight children as a problem,' she said.

'Little fat babies are loved and thought to be healthy. Parents are very proud that their children are a bit cuddly. Because they are fat when they are little, they grow up into little fat kindergarten children, become fat primary school children and this goes on.'

Busy fast food restaurants are part of the problem. With both parents often working full-time, the traditional Chinese diet is being swapped for fast foods. As well as eating junk snacks, many children do not get regular exercise. Hong Kong is one of the most over-crowded cities in the world and there aren't many playing fields.

Dr Ip says most children spend their free time indoors. 'They sit in front of the television or in front of the computer. They get a lift in a car to school and back home,' she says.

'All the high rise flats have fantastic fast lifts so they don't have to walk upstairs or downstairs.'

Medals for fitness

The schools have started a special awards scheme to try to persuade children to get fit. Children train for regular tests in running, sit-ups and other exercises, winning medals if they pass.

Teacher Carmen Li has entered all her pupils in the scheme. But even so, about a third of them are still fat. 'Hong Kong students have too many snacks, which can be bought everywhere,' she says. 'They will eat all day long. Some of them will eat during their lessons.'

But getting fit could be the difference between life and death. Heart attacks are now affecting those in their thirties and forties.

Questions

1 What does the term obese mean?

2 What similarities are there between the diet of children in Hong Kong and your diet?

3 Imagine you have a pen friend in Hong Kong who is obese. Write him/her a letter explaining how they should look after themselves to avoid health problems.

Remember

Write these rules in your exercise book.

- Being a little overweight is not the same as being obese (very fat).
- The only successful way to lose weight is to be careful what you eat and take regular exercise.
- Crash diets do not work!
- In your teens your body is undergoing a lot of changes.

In one end, out the other

It can take 24 hours for food to pass through your body. On its journey it is broken down. Useful chemicals are **absorbed** into the blood and taken around the body. Anything that we eat that our body doesn't need right away is either stored or **excreted** as waste. Figure 1 shows you what the human digestive system is like.

The digestive system

Stage 1

First we break up food by chewing it. We use our teeth to cut, slice and grind the food. The saliva in the mouth begins to break down any starch and changes it to sugar.

Stage 2

Then we swallow our food and it passes down the oesophagus or gullet. This is a tube of muscle that squeezes the food down into the stomach.

Stage 3

The food is now in the stomach. It is mixed with hydrochloric acid made by the stomach. This acid helps to break the food down. There are also other chemicals called **enzymes** in the stomach, these help to break down the food as well. By now the food has been turned into a liquid. It is squirted into the small intestine.

Stage 4

In the small intestine (or ileum), **bile** from the liver stops the fat clumping together. More enzymes are added to break down what is left of the food. The broken down food is absorbed into the bloodstream. The small intestine of a normal adult is nearly 7 metres long, so it's a long journey!

Stage 5

When it reaches the large intestine all the useful parts of the food have been absorbed. All that is left is waste, fibre and water. Because water is so important, the large intestine absorbs it back into the bloodstream so that all that's left is nearly solid waste. We get rid of this waste at regular intervals through the rectum and anus.

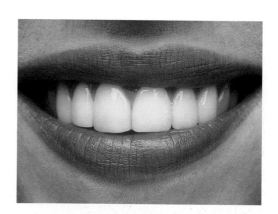

Figure 2 The teeth and saliva in the mouth begin to digest the food.

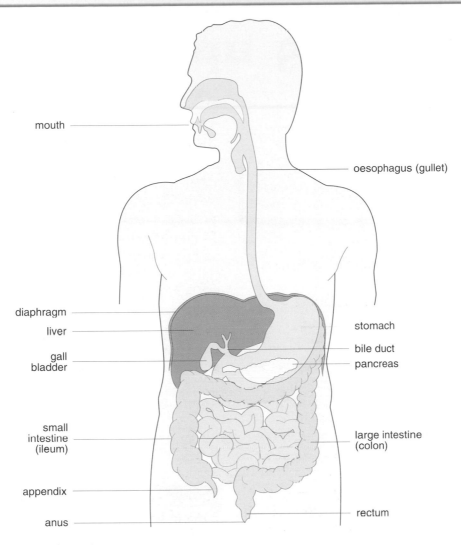

mouth

oesophagus (gullet)

diaphragm

liver

stomach

gall
bladder

bile duct

pancreas

small
intestine
(ileum)

large intestine
(colon)

appendix

rectum

anus

Figure 1 The human digestive system.

1 Describe what happens to a chip when you eat it and as it passes through your digestive system. (You could make this into a cartoon strip if you wanted to.)

2 What two things are added to the food in the stomach to help break the food down?

3 It can take up to 24 hours to fully digest a meal. Why do you think it takes this long and why is this a good thing?

Copy the following paragraph into your exercise book.

Digestion starts in the mouth and carries on in the stomach. Most digestion takes place in the small intestine. Useful chemicals from our food are absorbed into the bloodstream and transported around the body. Waste from our food has any useful water taken out of it and is pushed out of the body through the rectum. Digestion can take up to 24 hours to complete.

Breaking up is hard to do

Enzymes

The food that we eat may taste nice, look nice and smell nice, but we have to break it down in order for it to be of any use to us. When we eat something, chemicals in the stomach and small intestine break the food into simpler particles that our bodies can use. These chemicals are called enzymes.

Questions

1 What is an enzyme?

2 What two places in the body add enzymes to our food?

A balanced diet

If you remember from page 2 there are different food groups, and a balanced diet means we eat the right amount of each group.

Carbohydrates

There are two types of carbohydrates – starches and sugars.

Starch is a large molecule made up of lots of small sugar molecules. It doesn't dissolve easily. It is found in foods like rice, pasta and potatoes.

There are lots of different types of sugars. The most useful for us is glucose. This is the type of sugar that gives us energy. (A quick tip: chemicals whose name ends in **ose**, e.g. gluc**ose**, sucr**ose**, fruct**ose** and lact**ose** are all different types of sugar.) Sucrose is the sugar that we sprinkle into tea or on our food. Glucose is used in some fizzy drinks. Fructose is the sugar that makes fruits taste sweet. Lactose is found in milk. (You could keep a list at the back of your book of all the different types of sugars you come across.)

Figure 1 Starch and sugar are both carbohydrates.

Proteins

Proteins are body building foods. We need proteins for our muscles and to repair damaged tissues. We get proteins from eating meat and vegetables.

Figure 2 Protein is found in meat, nuts and vegetables.

Fats

We use fats to give us energy when we have run out of glucose.

Figure 3 Lard is made from animal fat.

Vitamins and minerals

Vitamins and minerals are very small compared to the other foods we have seen. They don't need to be broken down. They pass quite easily through the wall of the small intestine into our blood stream. Fruits and vegetables are a good source of vitamins and minerals.

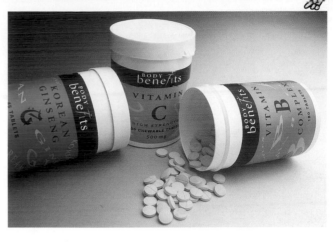

Figure 4 You can get extra vitamins and minerals from tablets like these.

There's a hole in my stomach Dr Beaumont!

Key words

gastric juice   Acidic liquid in the stomach that helps to digest food

How we digest our food was discovered after someone was shot! Read the following amazing story of how Dr William Beaumont found out how we digest our food, then answer the questions.

American Army surgeon, treated him, but he couldn't get the hole in St Martin's stomach to close over. For a while, the hole had to be covered to prevent food and drink from coming out when St Martin was eating.

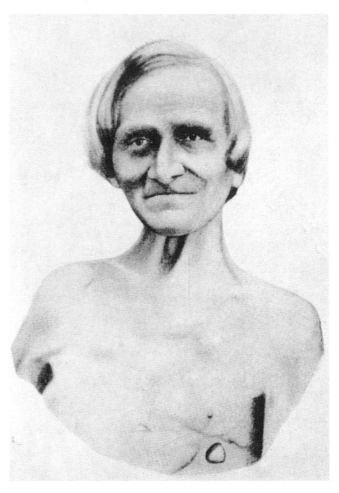

Figure 2 Alexis St Martin. You can clearly see the 'hole' on the left-hand side of his body.

Figure 1 Dr William Beaumont, who discovered how we digest food in our stomachs.

On 6 June 1822, in America, a fur trader called Alexis St Martin was accidentally shot. It left a hole in his stomach that was bigger than the palm of your hand. Dr William Beaumont, an

On 1 August 1825, Dr Beaumont decided to try some experiments on St Martin. Dr Beaumont was the first person to see digestion happening in the stomach. He tied pieces of food to the end of a silk string and dangled the food through the hole into St Martin's stomach.

He would pull out the string one hour, two hours and three hours later to see what had happened to the food. Five hours after he first put the food into St Martin's stomach, Beaumont removed it because St Martin was suffering from indigestion.

On 7 August 1825, Beaumont stopped St Martin eating for 17 hours. He took the temperature of St Martin's stomach – it was 37°C. He then took some **gastric juice** from St Martin's stomach, put it into a test tube and then found out how long a piece of corned beef took to dissolve in the test tube. He found that it took 10 hours. He also put another piece of meat of the same size into St Martin's stomach. His stomach digested the meal in two hours.

Digestion is when food is broken down into smaller particles. This happens so that food can be absorbed into the bloodstream. Dr Beaumont proved that part of this process happens in the stomach.

The food in the stomach is mixed with gastric juice. This is very acidic. It contains lots of hydrochloric acid. Gastric juice helps the enzymes in the stomach to break down the food.

Dr Beaumont also found that the digestive enzymes work best at body temperature, which is 37°C. They still work at lower temperatures, but they work more slowly.

Questions

1 Dr Beaumont looked at digestion in St Martin's stomach. Where else in the body does digestion happen?

2 Write out a simple method for Dr Beaumont's first experiments on St Martin.
   a) What was he doing that made his experiment a fair test?
   b) What variables was he trying to control in his first experiment?
   c) What variable(s) couldn't he control?

Questions

3 What kind of acid is found in the stomach?

4 What is body temperature?

Remember

Copy and complete the sentences. Use these words:

gastric   stomach   body   food

Digestion happens in the **s**_____.

Digestion is breaking down food into simpler substances that can be absorbed into the blood. The **f**_____ is broken down by **g**_____ juices. Digestive enzymes work best at **b**_____ temperature.

Finishing off!

Remember

Copy and complete the following paragraph using these words:

**minerals   food   fibre   fats
small intestine   bloodstream**

In order to grow, stay healthy and have energy we need **f**_____. The food we eat is broken down in our stomach and our **s**_____ **i**_____. It is then transported around the body by our **b**_____. The chemicals that make up our food can be put into seven groups:

1   carbohydrates

2   proteins

3   **f**____

4   vitamins

5   **m**_____

6   water

7   **f**_____.

Choose the correct word from the pairs below and copy the completed paragraph into your exercise book.

Digestion starts in the **throat/mouth**. It carries on in the stomach, but most digestion takes place in the **large intestine/small intestine**. Special chemicals called **enzymes/minerals** break up the food so that it can be absorbed into our blood and transported around the body. Waste from our food has any useful water taken from it and is pushed out of our body through the rectum. Digestion can take up to **72/24** hours to complete.

Question

1   Take a new page in your exercise book. Make a list of all the key words from the boxes in this chapter down the side. Take two lines per word. Try to write the meaning of each word without looking. Then go back and fill in any you did not know or got wrong. Now learn to spell them using the look–say–cover–spell method.

Web sites to visit:

William Beaumont
http://www.james.com/beaumont/dr_life.htm

12

Building blocks

Starter Activity
Putting the parts together

Cooking is about making the best mixture possible. Imagine eating the things for making a trifle on their own. You would eat dry sponge cake, then jelly cubes, then water, then custard powder, then whipped cream. It's much better as a mixture!

Science is about making good mixtures, just like trifle.

Questions

1 The word 'pure' has lots of different meanings. What do you think 'pure' means to a scientist? (*Hint*: chemical particles)

2 Air is a mixture of substances. Can you think of three different substances found in air?

3 How could you separate salt from broken glass? (*Hint*: use water)

4 What do the words solute, solvent and solution mean?

5 Both *melting* and *dissolving* make liquids. Explain the difference between the two words.

6 Black ink is not a pure substance. Its colours can be separated by using chromatography. Draw pictures to show how this could be done.

Tiny atoms

Key words

atom   A tiny particle of matter

compound   A pure substance made from more than one type of atom

element   A substance made from all the same type of atoms

mixture   Several substances together which can be separated

molecule   A particle made from atoms joined together

particles   The tiny pieces which make a substance

pure   Made from only one substance

Figure 1 Atoms seen under a very powerful microscope. The atoms look a bit like fuzzy round balls.

Everything can be made into smaller and smaller bits until you get down to things called **atoms**. An atom is the smallest **particle** of matter that you can have.

Elements, mixtures and compounds

Mixtures are things that can be separated into different **pure** substances. For example, salt water is a mixture. Pure substances are a much harder idea to understand.

Pure substances are those where all the particles are exactly the same.

Pure substances can be divided into two types:

1   **Elements** are pure substances where all the atoms are the same type.
2   **Compounds** are pure substances where different atoms are put together to make the same type of particle. These particles made from groups of atoms are called **molecules**.

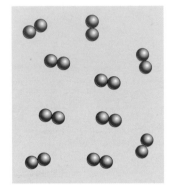

a) Oxygen   b) Carbon dioxide

Figure 2

Look at Figure 2. Oxygen on the left is an element. It contains only oxygen atoms, but the atoms 'go round in pairs' to make oxygen molecules.

Carbon dioxide on the right contains carbon atoms (the black circles) and oxygen atoms (the red circles) so it is a compound. All carbon dioxide molecules contain one carbon atom joined to two oxygen atoms.

Question

1   What do these words mean:
    a)   atom
    b)   element
    c)   compound?

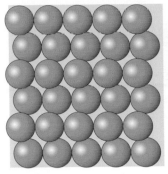
a) Copper

b) Copper oxide

Figure 3

Look at Figure 3. Copper on the left is an element. The copper atoms are in a regular pattern because it is a solid. Copper oxide on the right is a compound. Copper oxide is made of copper atoms (the brown circles) and oxygen atoms (the red circles). There is one oxygen atom joined to every copper atom.

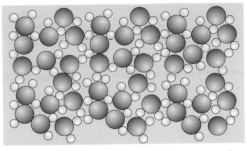

(iii) *Hint*: random jumble, little groups of particles are all the same.

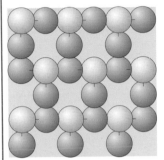

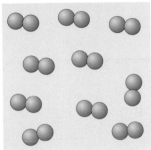

(iv) *Hint*: regular pattern, two different particles joined together to make one unit.

(v) *Hint*: widely spaced, only one type of particle.

Questions

2 Water molecules have two hydrogen atoms and one oxygen atom. Draw a particle picture of water vapour. Use the particle pictures in Figure 2 and 3 to help you. Make the hydrogen atoms white and the oxygen atoms red.

3 Look at the particle pictures below.
 a) Say if each one is a solid, liquid or gas.
 b) Say if each one shows an element, compound or mixture?

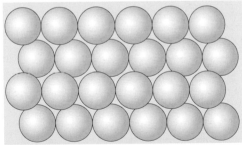

(i) *Hint*: regular pattern, only one particle.

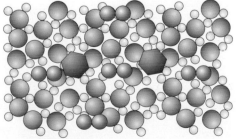

(ii) *Hint*: random jumble, different particles.

Remember

Solve these clues:

A pure substance – but not an element.

   co _ _ _ _ _ d (8 letters)

Joins with oxygen to make water.

   _ y _ rogen (8 letters)

The smallest particle that can exist on its own.

   _ t _ m (4 letters)

Most of the air.

   ni _ _ _ g _ n (8 letters)

A state of matter that can squash.

   _ _ s (3 letters)

A substance made of lots of the same atom.

   _ l _ m _ _ t (7 letters)

A list of elements

Key words

nucleus   The central part of an atom (do not confuse this with the nucleus that controls a living cell)

Periodic Table   This is a list of all the elements we know

symbol   Each element has an international symbol as well as a name

There are just over 100 elements, but only 90 of these are found naturally in the Earth's crust. Just the first 20 elements are shown in Figure 1 with their **symbols**.

Hydrogen gas was used to make the Hindenberg airship lighter than air. It burns very fiercely

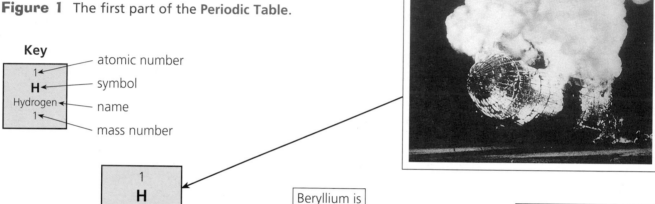

Figure 1 The first part of the **Periodic Table**.

Key

1	atomic number
H	symbol
Hydrogen	name
1	mass number

1
H
Hydrogen
1

Beryllium is found in the gemstone blue beryl

Boron is used to set fire to rockets

Hard diamonds and soft graphite (in pencil leads) are both made from carbon

Lithium is used in camera batteries

3	4
Li	**Be**
Lithium	Beryllium
7	9

Sodium metal is solid. Sodium is used in street lights

11	12
Na	**Mg**
Sodium	Magnesium
23	24

19	20
K	**Ca**
Potassium	Calcium
39	40

5	6
B	**C**
Boron	Carbon
10	12

13	14
Al	**Si**
Aluminium	Silicon
27	28

Silicon is used in computer memory circuits

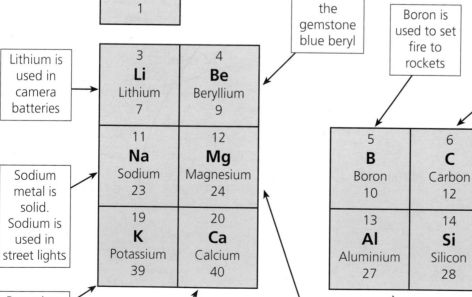

Potassium is used in fertilisers. Plants need potassium to grow

Marble is a very hard form of calcium carbonate

Magnesium is a very light metal. It is used to make pencil sharpeners and racing car wheels

Kitchen foil is made from aluminium

Atoms

Atoms are very small. One hundred million atoms in a line would fit into 1 cm. Atoms are fuzzy at the edges. The middle of an atom is called a **nucleus**.

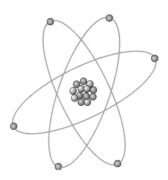

Figure 2 An atom.

Questions

1 Name three elements from the Periodic Table which are gases?

2 Name three elements which are metals?

3 Which gas is used to fill light bulbs? Why is it used for this job?

4 Which element is used in computer memory?

Remember

Copy and complete the sentences.

90   100 000 000   Periodic Table

There are _____ atoms in a line 1 cm long.

Only ___ elements are found naturally. These are listed in the **P_____ T_____**.

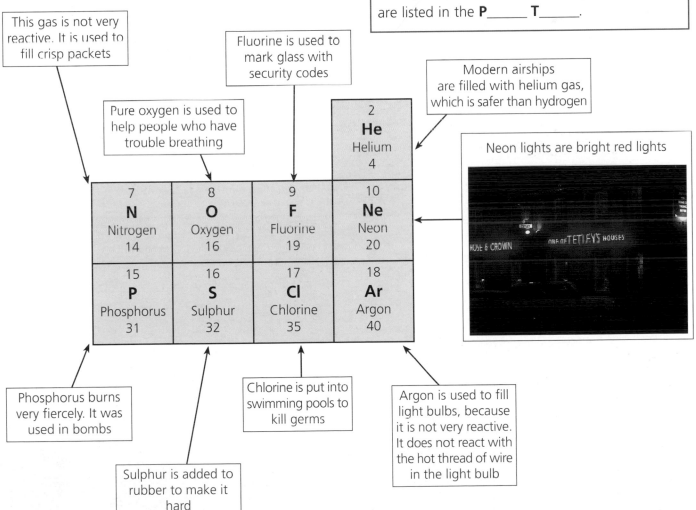

This gas is not very reactive. It is used to fill crisp packets

Fluorine is used to mark glass with security codes

Pure oxygen is used to help people who have trouble breathing

Modern airships are filled with helium gas, which is safer than hydrogen

Neon lights are bright red lights

			2 **He** Helium 4
7 **N** Nitrogen 14	8 **O** Oxygen 16	9 **F** Fluorine 19	10 **Ne** Neon 20
15 **P** Phosphorus 31	16 **S** Sulphur 32	17 **Cl** Chlorine 35	18 **Ar** Argon 40

Phosphorus burns very fiercely. It was used in bombs

Sulphur is added to rubber to make it hard

Chlorine is put into swimming pools to kill germs

Argon is used to fill light bulbs, because it is not very reactive. It does not react with the hot thread of wire in the light bulb

Multi metal

Key words

conduct   Allows energy to pass through it
metal   Material that conducts electricity easily and has lots of other useful properties

Metals are very useful materials. There are many different metals. We use metals to do lots of different jobs that can't be done any other way.

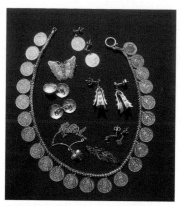

Figure 1   Gold is used for jewellery because it stays shiny.

Figure 2   Iron is used for bridges because it is very strong.

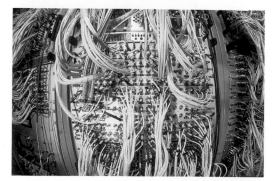

Figure 3   Copper is used for electric cables because it conducts electricity well and is flexible.

Figure 4   Brass is used for electric plugs and switches because it conducts electricity well and is hard.

Figure 5   Stainless steel is used for saucepans. It is strong and conducts energy well.

Figure 6   Silver is used for cutlery. It does not react with the food.

Figure 7   Aluminium is very flexible and it can be rolled out into thin sheets.

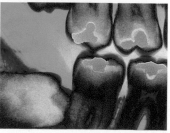

Figure 8   Mercury is used in tooth fillings.

Testing for metals

There are two good ways of testing a material to see if it is a metal.

1   Use a simple circuit with a battery and a light bulb. If the material put into the circuit **conducts** electricity and the bulb lights, it is a metal.

2   Hold the material in your hand. If it is a metal it feels cold. Metals are good conductors of heat. They will conduct the warmth from the hand away from the surface and so they continue to feel cold. (Try this with the head and handle of a hammer.)

Figure 9 The head of the hammer will feel colder than the handle because it is made of metal.

Questions

1   Make a list of 10 different metals you can think of.

2   Make a list of metal objects that you own. Try to add the name of the metal they are made of.

3   What metals are the Olympic medals made from. What does each metal look like?

Remember

Use these words to fill in the gaps:

electricity   conductors

Metals are good c_____ of heat. Metals can conduct enough e_____ to light a bulb.

Dirty work

Toby wanted to clean his uncle's darts trophies. He washed and polished the plastic and wood ones. He used special metal cleaning stuff on the metal ones. The metal ones came up really shiny even though the surface started off very dull.

Figure 10 Which is which?

He was puzzled about what to use on two of the trophies. One was made of 'pewter' and one was made of 'bakelite'. Both were black, dull and dirty.

Toby had no idea what cleaning method to use on them. He tested them and here are his results.

	Heat of hand test	Electrical test
Pewter	Felt cold for a long time	Conducted electricity: bulb lit up
Bakelite	Quickly felt warm	Did not conduct: bulb stayed unlit

Table 1 Toby's results

Questions

4   Which trophy was metal?

5   What would the metal trophy look like when clean?

Metals and non-metals

What makes metals useful?

All metals have **properties** that make them similar to each other.

The less important ones are:

● they are shiny if the surface is clean.
● they make a nice 'ting' if hit.

The more important ones are:

● they are tough.
● they do not shatter.
● they can be shaped by squashing them.
● they do not crack easily.
● they can hold large weights without breaking.
● they don't melt easily (except mercury).
● some metals are magnetic. Iron and steel are strongly magnetic. Cobalt and nickel are weakly magnetic.
● they conduct energy easily.
● they conduct electricity well.

The main difference between one metal and another is how heavy it is and how quickly it reacts or **corrodes**.

Figure 1   A steel knife is tough (does not wear away or crack) and strong (thin, but does not bend out of shape).

Figure 2   Tungsten is a metal. A tungsten filament (a very thin thread) in a light bulb conducts electricity well and has a very high melting point.

Question

1   Copy the first column of the table below. Sort out the second column so that the correct property is next to the correct metal.

Metal	Property
copper	very hard, used for aeroplanes
gold	very light, used for window frames
aluminium	stays shiny, used for jewellery
titanium	liquid metal, used in thermometers
Mercury	conducts electricity well, used for wires

Non-metals

There are only about 20 elements that are **non-metals**. They also have certain properties.

- Many are gases. The others all have low melting points.
- They are brittle if they are solid.
- They do not conduct heat well.
- They do not conduct electricity well.

a) Carbon

b) Sulphur

c) Chlorine

d) Oxygen

e) Nitrogen

f) Phosphorus

Figure 3 Non-metal elements are different colours and some are gases.

Questions

2 Look at the pictures of the elements in Figure 3.
  a) Which are gases?
  b) Are the solids shiny like metals?

3 Copy the table below and match each non-metal with its correct use.

Non-metallic element	Use
carbon	very light gas, used in balloons
chlorine	gas we use in our bodies which is taken in by the lungs
helium	barbecue charcoal; burns well to give lots of heat
oxygen	kills germs in water supply and swimming pools

Very few of the non-metals are useful materials in the way that metals are. All their usefulness comes from their chemical reactions.

Remember

Copy and complete the sentences. Use these words:

**low   brittle   crack   gases   shiny
not   conduct   magnetic**

Metal elements are **s**_____, they do not **c**_____ easily, some are **m**_____. They **c**_____ electricity well.

Non-metallic elements are not tough, they are **b**_____. They are **g**_____ or **l**_____ melting point solids. They do **n**____ conduct electricity well.

Making compounds

combine Join together chemically so they can't be separated easily

limestone A common type of rock

methane Natural gas

rearranged Put into new groups without losing any atoms

Atoms join together to form compounds. In compounds, the clusters of atoms are called molecules. Each molecule is exactly the same. There are rules for making compounds.

Rules

1 If metal atoms form a compound, they have to **combine** with non-metal atoms.

2 Non-metal atoms can combine with other non-metal atoms to make the molecules of a compound.

3 Molecules usually contain small numbers of atoms. Carbon atoms don't follow this rule. They can make really big molecules.

4 When new molecules are formed, the atoms don't vanish or get made from nothing. They just get **rearranged**.

a) Water: two hydrogen atoms joined to an oxygen atom.

b) **Methane** (natural gas): four hydrogen atoms joined to a carbon atom.

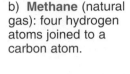

c) Sand: a silicon atom and two oxygen atoms (silicon dioxide).

d) **Limestone**: a calcium atom and three oxygen atoms joined to a carbon atom (calcium carbonate).

e) Carbon dioxide: a carbon atom with two oxygen atoms joined to it.

Figure 1

1 Compounds such as methane are pure substances. Explain why.

2 What is the name of a cluster of atoms joined together?

3 In equations, water molecules are written as H_2O. This is called their formula. Explain what the formula of water means.

Burning methane

Figure 2 A Bunsen burner burns methane in oxygen to produce carbon dioxide and water

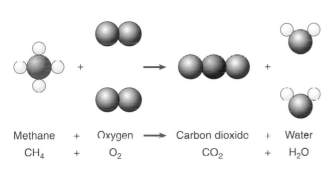

| Methane | + | Oxygen | $\longrightarrow$ | Carbon dioxide | + | Water |
| CH_4 | + | O_2 | | CO_2 | + | H_2O |

Figure 3 The atoms involved in the reaction between methane and oxygen.

When methane burns, the hydrogen atoms get pinched first to make water molecules. Then the carbon atoms in the methane combine with oxygen to make carbon dioxide gas.

Questions

4   What solution do you use to test for carbon dioxide?

5   What do you see during the test if carbon dioxide is present?

6   What substance other than carbon dioxide is made when methane burns?

Testing a gas: carbon dioxide

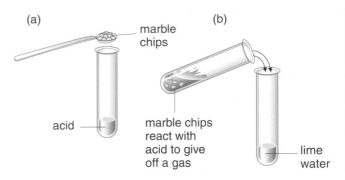

a) Put calcium carbonate chips into some acid.

b) When the test tube fills up, pour the gas into a test tube containing a little limewater.

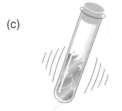 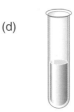

c) Shake the limewater and the gas.

d) If the limewater goes milky, the gas is carbon dioxide.

Figure 4

Remember

Copy and complete the sentences. Use these words:

**molecules   compounds   atoms
combine**

Atoms **c**_____ with each other to make new substances called **c**_____. New particles made in this way are often called **m**_____.

When chemical changes happen, the **a**_____ get rearranged into different molecules and no atoms get lost.

Oil and gas

Petroleum is the proper name for 'crude oil' that is found **underground**. There is more petroleum on Earth than any other liquid, except for water. Crude oil and natural gas are often found together. The natural gas is **dissolved** in the liquid oil.

Crude oil provides two-thirds of the world's energy supplies. The oil and gas are **non-renewable** sources. Our use of them has increased so much that we worry about how long they will last. The supplies will probably run out **this century**.

Crude oil is not a pure substance. It contains many different materials. Petrol, paraffin, **kerosene** (for aeroplane fuel), diesel fuel, engine oil and bitumen (road tar) are all found in crude oil.

People have used substances from crude oil for thousands of years. Some oil finds its way naturally up to the Earth's surface. Here it evaporates and leaves behind **bitumen** – the tarry part of the crude oil. This has been used for thousands of years as a **waterproofing agent** for plumbing, boat building and brick work.

In the history books it talks about bitumen being used as a coating for Moses' basket. Noah's Ark was waterproofed inside and out with it. The Native Americans collected crude oil to use in medicines. The American settlers learned to collect it to use as fuel in their lamps.

Crude oil became **valuable** in the nineteenth century. The whaling industry did not provide enough whale oil to light the lamps of the world and a new source was needed. The first oil well was drilled in August 1859.

The uses for oil increased as the supply grew. The car engine meant that the petrol from the oil mixture was needed for transport. Then the invention of aeroplanes needed more fuel which had to be supplied from oil. In the 1940s **man-made** materials (such as nylon and polythene) made from oil were invented.

It is no wonder that oil was called 'black gold' and that discovery of oil and gas could mean riches beyond belief.

Oil is a fossil fuel. When we burn it we are releasing energy captured from the Sun millions of years ago by **prehistoric** plants and animals. The remains of these **microscopic** plants and tiny animals settled on the sea bed. They were buried by sand as the years went by. The layers built up and the living things turned into oil. Some of this oil was trapped underground, not as a 'lake' but in the sandy rock itself.

An oil well is drilled to look for pockets of **porous** rock that contains the crude oil. When a pocket is found, water is pumped down to push the oil to the surface. The crude oil is then taken to a refinery. At the refinery the oil is separated into its parts by fractional distillation.

Figure 1 An oil refinery

Questions

1 Make a list of the 12 words or phrases in **bold** type and write their meanings beside them.

2 Write down all the uses of crude oil that are in the text. Add any more that you know about.

3 'Cars use energy from the Sun.' Explain why this is true.

CHAPTER 2

Finishing off!

The history of the Periodic Table

The Periodic Table is not an artificial arrangement of the elements; it is a true discovery. Like all discoveries, many people contributed to it.

1829 Johann Dobereiner
He made a list of all the elements in order of mass (how heavy they are).

1858 Stanislau Cannizzaro
He made a list of the atomic masses of the 60 known elements.

1864 John Newlands
He found a pattern of chemical properties when the elements were arranged in order of mass. People laughed at him and said alphabetical order would be better.

1869 Dimitri Mendeleyev
He was the best! He produced the first Periodic Table. He left gaps, predicting that elements would be discovered later.

1875
The element gallium was discovered, with the properties Mendeleyev had predicted.

1886
Germanium was found exactly as predicted.

1890
Helium, argon and neon were also found. A new group – Group 0 – was put in for them.

1913 Ernest Rutherford
He discovered that the atom had a central nucleus.

Henry Moseley
He found that when the elements were listed in atomic number order, they fell perfectly into place.

Now
We have added man-made elements like plutonium to the Periodic Table.

1 Take a new page in your exercise book. Make a list of all the Key Words from the boxes in this chapter down the side. Take two lines per word. Try to write the meaning of each word without looking. Then go back and fill in any you did not know or got wrong.

   Now learn to spell them by the look–say–cover–write method.

2 Look at the Periodic Table on page 151. Fill in a table with these headings, making it as long as possible.

Elements I have heard of	Metal or non-metal	What I know about them

Web sites to visit:

Web elements – Periodic Table
   http://www.shef.ac.uk/~chem/web-elements/

Metals and Non-metals
   http://student.biology.arizona.edu/sciconn/Metals/Metals.html

Energy transfers

Starter Activity
Staying warm and going cold

Make a warm drink and forget about it for half an hour and you will find it has gone cold. Your body is warm. If you forget about it for half an hour it will stay warm.

Both you and the drink transfer energy to your surroundings. A hot drink warms the things around it. So does your body. The difference is that you take in food. Food is your fuel and your energy resource. When you eat the food, you replace the energy you lose to your surroundings. The drink can't replace the energy it loses.

The drink has a starting temperature of 50°C, and a finishing temperature of 20°C

The girl has a starting temperature of 37°C, and a finishing temperature of 37°C

Questions

1 What is the name of the unit that we use for measuring temperature?

2 Look at the picture above. How much did the temperature of the drink change?

3 Why does the drink cool down and you don't?

4 What is the temperature on the Celsius scale at which ice melts?

5 What is the temperature on the Celsius scale at which water boils?

6 Name three different fuels that are burned in people's houses?

7 Name two fuels that cars and lorries use.

8 What is a 'fossil' fuel?

9 Where does coal come from (as a raw material)?

10 Where do humans get their energy from?

11 Where do plants get their energy from?

Temperature differences

Figure 1 A letterbox in a) winter and b) summer

Energy can transfer into and out of objects, depending on the temperature difference between them and their surroundings.

Winter or summer, a letterbox is just a lump of metal in a useful shape. It doesn't actually *do* anything itself. But its temperature changes. It changes when the temperature of its surroundings changes.

Early in the morning the letterbox is cool. The Sun warms the air which is then at a higher temperature than the letterbox. Energy transfers into the letterbox.

In the evening the air turns cooler so the letterbox will also turn cooler as energy transfers away from it. Energy doesn't transfer in or out when the temperature of the letterbox is the same as the temperature of the surroundings.

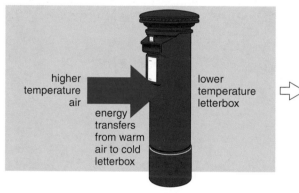
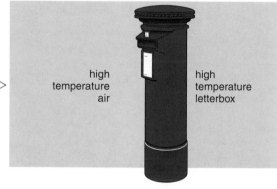

Figure 2 a) Energy transfers into the letterbox when the air is at a higher temperature (warmer) than the letterbox.

b) No temperature difference – no overall energy transfer.

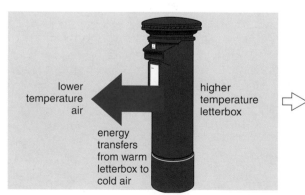
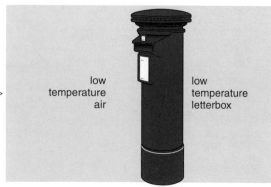

Figure 3 a) Energy transfers out of the letterbox when the air is at a lower temperature than the letterbox.

b) No temperature difference – no overall energy transfer.

Other objects behave in the same way as the letterbox.

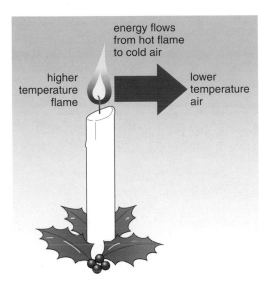

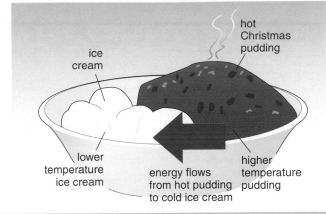

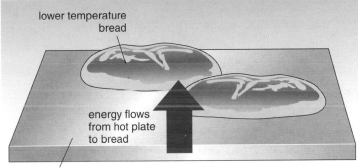

Figure 4 The arrows show the overall energy transfer. When there is a temperature difference between two objects in contact, the cold one gains energy, the hot one loses energy.

Questions

1 What would happen to the temperature of a letterbox when it snows if
  a) the snow is warmer than the letterbox is to start with?
  b) the snow is colder than the letterbox is to start with?

2 Sketch energy transfer diagrams for
  a) an ice cube floating in a glass of lemonade
  b) a pile of cold oven chips when you put them into a hot oven
  c) a bottle of warm milk that's just been moved from a warm room into a fridge.

Remember

Copy and complete the sentences. Use these words:

lower   higher   same   energy temperature

Energy transfer takes place when there is a **t**___ difference. The **e**___ transfer takes place from the object at the **h**___ temperature to the object at the **l**___ temperature. Energy transfer is in balance when the objects have the **s**___ temperature.

Energy transfers and temperature

energy balance   There is no overall energy transfer

global climate change   A change in the Earth's weather, caused by a change in average temperature

Energy from the Sun arrives at planets like Venus, Earth and Mars. The energy warms the planets' surfaces. Planets also transfer energy back out into space.

A warm planet radiates energy out into space. Each of the planets is in **energy balance**. Energy arrives at the same rate as it leaves. Each of the planets has its own natural average temperature. This temperature doesn't change unless the atmosphere of the planet changes.

On Earth, humans are changing the atmosphere. This could change the Earth's average temperature and cause **global climate change**.

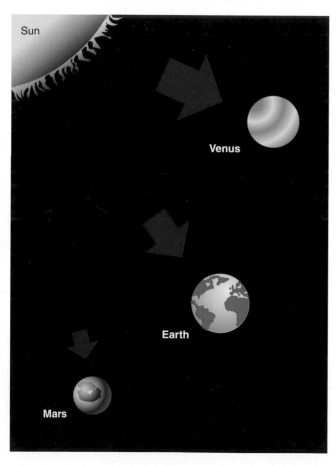

Figure 1   The light of the Sun warms the Earth and other planets like Venus and Mars. Venus is closer to the Sun than we are. It receives more energy from the Sun than the Earth does. Mars is further away from the Sun so the energy that it receives is less.

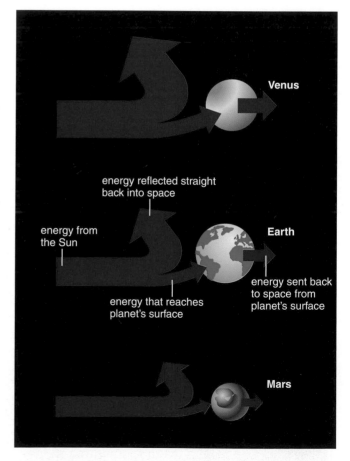

Figure 2   Mars, Venus and Earth receive energy from the Sun. Some of the energy that arrives at each planet is reflected straight back into space. Some of the energy warms each planet's surface.

Climate change

These energy transfer diagrams show how a planet's temperature can change.

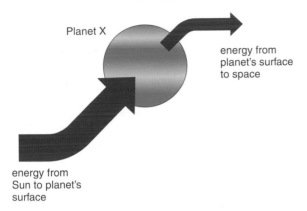

Planet X

energy from planet's surface to space

energy from Sun to planet's surface

Figure 3 If a planet's surface receives more energy than it sends back into space, it gets hotter and hotter – its average temperature rises.

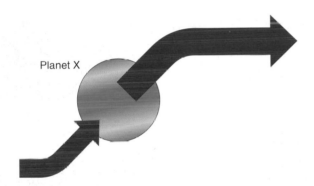

Planet X

Figure 4 If a planet's surface sends more energy out into space than it receives from the Sun, it becomes colder – its average temperature falls.

Figure 5 Tim Docherty is a climate scientist. He is studying the effect of pollution on our climate.

Questions

1 What does energy balance mean?

2 Which one of these planets is in energy balance?

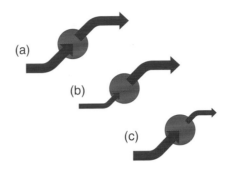

(a)

(b)

(c)

3 What will happen to the temperature of a planet if:
a) energy arrives at the planet faster than it leaves?
b) energy leaves faster than it arrives?

Remember

Copy and complete the sentences. Use these words:

Mars   same   planets   Sun   balance   temperature   space   atmosphere

Energy transfers out from the **S____**. Some energy reaches **p_____** like Venus, Earth and **M____**. The warmed planets send energy back out into **s____**. The amounts of energy they receive and the energy they send back out are the **s____**. They are in energy **b____**. Each planet stays at a steady temperature. But if the **a____** of a planet changes, then it could lose energy more slowly. This would cause the average **t____** of the planet to rise.

Warm bodies in cold places

Human bodies are usually warmer than their surroundings. They transfer energy into their surroundings. This energy must be replaced. If we live in cold places we must slow down this energy transfer.

Jane Mitchell is a scientist who has worked in the Antarctic. She is helping us to find out more about our planet.

Antarctica is a huge continent around the South Pole. Almost all of it is covered in ice. Even in summer the weather is far too cold for snow to melt. In winter it is dark nearly all of the time, and the blizzards last for days.

Twenty people live and work at the research station in the Antarctic. Fresh supplies have to be carried on sledges from a ship 15 kilometres away. When Jane went on trips outside the station, two things were really important – plenty of food and special warm clothing.

Our body temperature has to stay close to 37°C. If it doesn't, we die. The bigger the temperature difference between our body temperature and the temperature around us, the faster the energy flows from our body. In Antarctica where the temperatures are very low, the energy can transfer out very quickly indeed. Good clothes provide **insulation**. Energy can only transfer out through them very slowly.

We also have to replace the energy we lose. We eat food to replace the energy. Food carries a store of energy. The energy was stored in the food by plants, using the light of the Sun. Jane and the other scientists in the Antarctic eat plenty of 'high energy' foods like rice, instant mashed potato and chocolate.

Figure 1 Jane Mitchell at the research station, finding out more about our world.

Figure 2 These energy stores can replace the energy that transfers out of our body into the cold world outside.

Figure 3 Early explorers, like the one of the left, had poor food and poor clothing. Their bodies couldn't cope with the cold. Modern scientists, like the person on the right, carry good energy stores like chocolate. They wear clothing that insulates them very well to reduce energy transfer.

Questions

1 What is the temperature of your body in °C?

2 What does 'insulation' mean?

3 Explain why cold weather can make you hungry.

Remember

Copy and complete the sentences. Use these words:

**warmer   transfers   insulate   energy
reduce   temperature**

We need food to supply our bodies with **e___**.

Our bodies are almost always **w____** than our surroundings. They are at a higher **t___**. In cold surroundings energy **t____** out from our body very quickly. Clothes **i___** us to **r___** the energy flow from our body.

Different energy transfers

Convection

One way to transfer energy from place to place is to actually move hot material from place to place. Hot water moves around central heating pipes to the radiators. It carries energy from the boiler. Heated material sometimes moves naturally.

Figure 1 The burner heats the air inside this balloon. The air in the balloon expands (gets bigger). This makes the hot air float in the surrounding cool air and it takes the whole balloon with it.

Another example of naturally transferring energy is when you open the door of a hot oven. You can feel the hot air rising as it floats up in the cool surrounding air. The hot air carries energy with it.

This natural transfer of heat also occurs in liquids like water.

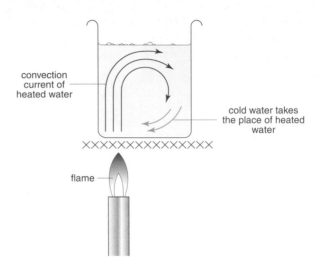

convection current of heated water

cold water takes the place of heated water

flame

Figure 2 A convection current in a liquid.

The hot parts of the liquid rise above the cooler parts of the liquid. Eventually the hot liquid cools and falls to take the place of the heated water. The transfer of energy by natural movement of a gas or liquid is called **convection**.

Evaporation

You are sweating in a car on a hot day. You open a window and the air rushing past cools you down rapidly.

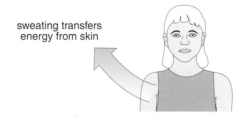

sweating transfers energy from skin

Figure 3 Sweating transfers energy from your skin.

The sweat (water) **evaporates** quickly and when it does it takes energy away from your skin. The faster the evaporation, the faster the energy transfers away from your skin.

Conduction

Imagine you are holding a metal rod with one end in a hot flame. Very soon the end you are holding will get very hot. The metal rod has transferred energy to your hand.

All materials are made of particles. The more energy the particles have, the faster they move. In solids, the particles are close together and there are strong forces between them, so fast particles with a lot of energy bounce off other particles nearby. They transfer some of their energy to the slower particles. In solids, energy can transfer quickly from particle to particle. Energy transferred in this way is transferred by **conduction**.

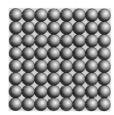

particles in a gas   particles in a solid

Figure 4 In solids there are more opportunities for particles to collide and interact.

In gases the particles are far apart. There aren't many opportunities for collisions. So gases are not very good at transferring energy by conduction.

Radiation

The Sun is so hot it glows white. It **radiates** energy to us across empty space. The filament inside a light bulb is not quite so hot, but it still radiates energy to us.

Much cooler objects also radiate energy. A brick radiates energy. You are warmer than the brick so you will radiate more energy than the brick, but not as much as the light bulb. Special infra-red cameras can 'see' this radiation. Rescue services use these cameras to help find people.

Figure 5 This photograph of firemen was taken by an infra-red camera.

Convection, evaporation, conduction and radiation are all types of **thermal** energy transfer. Thermal means to do with heating.

Questions

1 Name the four different ways in which energy can be transferred.

2 Which energy transfer can take place across space?

Remember

Copy and complete the sentences. Use these words:

evaporating   particles   convection   radiation   conduction   expands

When a liquid or gas is heated it **ex**_____.
This causes **c**_____ currents.

An **ev**_____ liquid takes energy from its surroundings.

In **c**_____ , energy transfers when **p**_____ collide with each other.

All hot bodies emit **r**_____.The radiation can travel across space.

Paying the bill for warmth

Warm houses transfer energy to their cool surroundings. This energy must be replaced. We use energy resources to keep us warm in our houses. We can burn a gas fire or a coal fire. We can use heaters that use electricity that has been generated in a power station. Our central heating might run on oil or gas, or it may use electricity. All of these energy resources cost money, and they all cause pollution.

Figure 1 Most energy resources are expensive. We must pay for the megajoules of energy we need every week to keep our house warm. (The joule is the unit of energy. A megajoule is a million joules.)

Reducing the bill

We want our house warm in winter when it is cold outside. The temperature difference makes energy transfer outwards rapidly. Energy flows out through the walls, roof and windows.

We need to control this flow if we want to stay warm and have a low fuel bill.

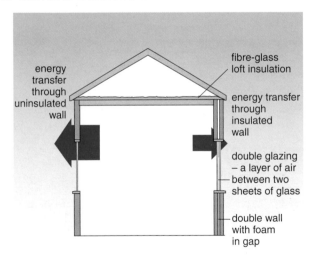

Figure 2 Fibre-glass reduces the flow of energy through the roof.

To control the energy transfer process we can insulate the roof space with fibre-glass wool. We can insulate the windows using heavy curtains and double glazing. These materials act as **thermal insulators**.

energy transfer through uninsulated wall

fibre-glass loft insulation

energy transfer through insulated wall

double glazing – a layer of air between two sheets of glass

double wall with foam in gap

Figure 3 The left hand side of the house has no extra insulation. Energy transfers outwards. Insulation materials reduce energy transfer on the right hand side of the house.

Questions

1 Name one unit of energy.

2 Describe two ways of saving money on heating bills.

Problems with pollution

Figure 4 Power stations release pollution into the atmosphere.

Burning fuels at home or in a power station causes pollution in the atmosphere. Coal, oil and gas are all fossil fuels. Sooner or later we will use up all the fossil fuels on Earth. Our atmosphere will become more polluted. Fortunately, if it is not too late, there are other energy resources available.

Solar energy

Solar energy is becoming more and more important. **Solar panels** generate electricity from the light of the Sun. They are a bit like the leaves of a plant. They soak up energy from the light.

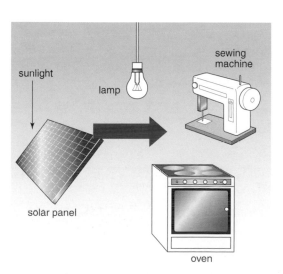

Figure 5 Solar energy can be used for lighting, cooking and running machinery.

Solar panels are getting better and cheaper. In some parts of the world, people are already using them for energy for cooking, lighting, heating and for running machinery.

Perhaps sunlight will replace fossil fuels as a main source of energy. Once you have the solar panels and the circuits to go with them, sunshine does not cost anything. It is a completely **renewable** fuel – it isn't going to run out. Unfortunately we do not get as much sunlight in winter.

Figure 6 A house of the future?

The house in Figure 6 uses solar panels to generate its electricity. It's also very well insulated to reduce the rate of transfer of energy out into its surroundings.

Question

3 Explain the advantages of solar energy over other energy resources for heating. What are the disadvantages?

Remember

Copy and complete the sentences. Use these words:

**coal   energy   temperature
oil   insulation   burn
renewable   gas   differences**

Temperature **d**____ cause energy transfer. The bigger the **t**____ difference, the faster the **e**____ transfer. We can control energy transfer with **i**____. Solar energy is **r**____. It will not run out. Fossil fuels, such as **c**____, **g**____ and **o**____ also produce pollution when we **b**____ them.

Finishing off!

Remember

★ The Sun's light carries energy. The Sun is the source of most of the Earth's energy resources.

★ The Sun's energy reaches us by radiation. This is the only way the energy from the Sun can travel through empty space.

★ An object has internal energy. When an object's temperature rises its internal energy rises.

★ Energy can transfer from one object to another.

★ During energy transfers, some heating of the material takes place. This makes the energy more 'spread out' (or dissipated.)

★ Energy that is spread out is difficult to use.

★ Energy can transfer by processes that include **convection**, **conduction** and **radiation**. **Evaporation** of material also results in energy transfer. These are all **thermal** energy transfers. Thermal means to do with heating.

★ **Insulation** resists thermal energy transfers.

★ **Solar panels** generate electricity from sunlight.

Questions

1 Take a new page in your exercise book. Make a list of all the Key Words from the boxes in this chapter down the side. Take two lines per word. Try to write the meaning of each word without looking. Then go back and fill in any you did not know or got wrong.

Now learn to spell them by the look–say–cover–write method.

2 Name the thermal energy transfer process used in the following situations:
  a) making toast
  b) cooking an egg in a frying pan
  c) heating a large pan of water.

3 All of the energy transfer processes in Question 2 transfer some energy to their surroundings. What happens to this energy?

4 a) Explain why a lot of energy is lost from a house through the windows and doors.
  b) Insulation material is put inside the walls to reduce energy loss. Explain how this works.
  c) Silvered paper is often put behind heating radiators which are on outside walls. Explain how this works.

5 To survive in mountains, people are told to dig a hole in the snow, get in and cover themselves with more snow to stay warm. Why does this work?

Web sites to visit:

CREATE – Centre for Research, Education & Training in Energy
http://www.create.org.uk

Planet Energy – information about renewable energy sources
http://www.dti.gov.uk/renewable/ed_pack

CHAPTER 4

Respiration

Some people exercise for fun. Others exercise to get fit. When we exercise we need a supply of energy. This chapter will look at how our body uses energy.

In school you will have PE lessons and do lots of different activities. They are all types of exercise.

Questions

1 Make a list of all the things you did in the past week that you would call exercise.

2 Think about the following types of exercise.
  ★ A five hour walk in the country
  ★ Two hours of dancing at a disco
  ★ An hour of football or hockey training
  ★ An hour and a half of helping at an old people's home, lifting and carrying.
  Which of these do you think is the best exercise to keep you healthy? Explain why you think that.

3 Different exercise has different effects on the body. What exercise do you think is best for:
  a) strength
  b) suppleness – being able to bend and twist with ease
  c) stamina – being able to exercise or play for a long time
  d) speed?

How do cells use food?

Key words

cellular respiration   Release of energy that happens in our cells

glucose   A type of sugar, used to produce energy in respiration

respiration   Releasing energy from fuels in the body

Figure 2 Glucose is our main source of energy.

Our main fuel that provides us with energy is **glucose**. Glucose is produced when carbohydrates (see page 2) from foods like bread and cereal are digested. Energy is released from glucose in the cells in our body in the same way as energy is released from other fuels. Oxygen reacts with the glucose, energy is released and carbon dioxide is produced. This reaction is called **respiration**. A simple equation for the reaction is shown below. When it happens in our cells it is called **cellular respiration**.

Figure 1 Exercising muscles need more energy.

Supermarkets and shops sell many different high energy foods and drinks. People like them if they are playing sports. The more we exercise, the more energy our muscles need.

Questions

1   Name three things that our body does that need energy.

2   Glucose is our main energy-giving chemical. What energy-giving chemical does a car use?

3   What happens to the carbon dioxide we produce in our cells?

4   What does the term cellular respiration mean?

Respiration:

glucose + oxygen → carbon dioxide + water +  ENERGY TRANSFER

Sports drinks – what are they?

Figure 3 Sports drinks.

Have you ever had a sports drink like the ones in Figure 3? As well as providing us with fuels to release energy, like glucose, they also contain chemical salts and water. When we exercise, as well as needing energy, we also need to replace water we lose by sweating. Sports drinks help to replace water quickly. It is important for us to replace lost water when we exercise as well as making sure that we drink plenty of water during the day.

When we sweat during exercise, our body is trying to keep our temperature at the right level. Heat produced by our muscles when we exercise can increase our body temperature. As the air evaporates the sweat from our skin, heat is lost. Try licking the back of your hand then blowing gently on the wet patch, it will feel cool.

Sweating means that we lose water and salts from our body. Try tasting some sweat by licking your hand next time you exercise. It will taste salty. Sports drinks not only replace the water, but also the salts you lose as well.

Questions

5   What three things do sports drinks contain?

6   Why do we sweat when we exercise?

Remember

Choose the correct word from the pairs below, then copy and complete the paragraph into your exercise book

Staying alive needs **stamina/energy**. Our main fuel, **glucose/petrol**, comes from the **minerals/food** we eat. In living cells, energy is released when **petrol/glucose** reacts with **nitrogen/oxygen** from the air we breathe. At the same time waste **urine/water** and **carbon dioxide/hydrogen** are produced. This chemical reaction is called **respiration/perspiration**

How does oxygen and glucose get to our cells?

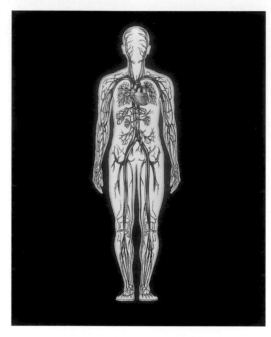

Figure 2 Blood moves in tubes to every part of our body.

Key words

plasma   The pale yellow coloured liquid part of blood

red blood cells   The cells in the blood that carry oxygen

Most of us know we have blood, but many people are not very sure of why we need it.

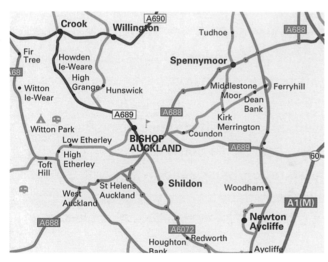

Figure 1 Cars and lorries move around roads to every part of the country.

Lorries move from one end of the country to the other. They deliver essential goods to all our cities, towns and villages. Blood is the main transport system in our body. An adult has about five litres of blood in his/her body. Oxygen and other substances, like glucose are moved around our body by blood. Respiration takes place in all of our cells, so blood has to reach all of them delivering glucose and oxygen.

Figure 3 This pack contains blood given by a donor. Notice that it has begun to separate out into yellow plasma and a red, thicker layer containing blood cells.

Blood looks like a thick red liquid. But it contains different types of cells and a pale yellow liquid called **plasma**. The **red blood cells** carry oxygen. There are about 5000 million red blood cells in every 1 cm³ of blood. As blood goes through the lungs, the red blood cells pick up oxygen from the air we breathe in. This oxygen is then released where it is needed as blood passes through tissues like muscles.

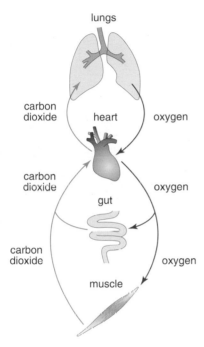

Figure 4 This shows how oxygen and carbon dioxide are transported around the body.

Blood also carries the glucose needed for respiration. The glucose is picked up by the blood vessels that surround our intestines. Glucose is then carried to the cells and moves into them. As blood circulates, or moves around the body, all the tissues will get oxygen and glucose.

Blood is mainly water and so it is very good at dissolving things. Waste carbon dioxide is produced during respiration. This gas dissolves in the plasma. The dissolved carbon dioxide is carried by blood to the lungs where it is released and breathed out.

4.3

How does blood get around?

Figure 2 William Harvey

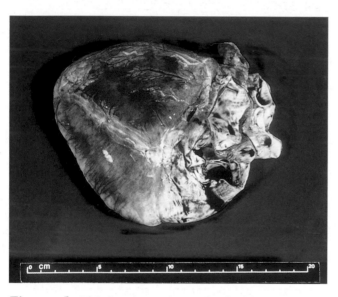

Key words

artery   Thick walled tubes that carry blood away from the heart

capillary   Very thin tubes that carry blood to the tissues of the body

vein   Thin walled tubes that carry blood back to the heart

Figure 1   This is what a heart looks like. It's one of the hardest working muscles in your body so it needs a good blood supply of its own.

In 1628, an English doctor called William Harvey showed that blood moves constantly around the body in one direction.

Blood has to be moved to and from every part of your body. It is the heart that makes this possible. The heart walls are made from muscle that contracts, or beats, all the time. It pumps blood through tubes called blood vessels from the heart and back to it again. You can tell how hard your heart is working by measuring your pulse. You can feel your pulse in your wrist or in your neck.

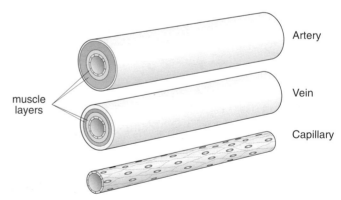

Artery

Vein

muscle layers

Capillary

Figure 3   *Arteries* have thick walls and take blood *away* from the heart. *Veins* have thinner walls and take blood *back to* the heart. *Capillaries* are tubes with very thin walls. They join arteries to veins.

There are three main types of blood vessels, **arteries**, **veins** and **capillaries**.

The heart has two pumps that work together. One side pumps blood to the lungs, the other side pumps blood to the rest of the body.

Questions

1 The heart muscle has its own blood supply.
   a) Why do you think the heart needs a supply of oxygen?
   b) What do you think would happen if the arteries in the heart were blocked?

Blood is pumped through arteries, away from the heart, to the body. The blood in arteries contains lots of oxygen. The arteries get narrower and narrower until they form a network of capillaries. Capillaries have thin walls and are very close to our cells. Because the capillaries are so near to the cells, chemicals can move easily between the blood in the capillaries and the cells. The veins take the blood from the cells back to the heart. The blood in veins contains waste carbon dioxide.

If we could take all of the blood vessels out of a child's body and lay them end to end, they would stretch for over 60,000 miles. An adult's blood vessels would stretch to over 100,000 miles. That's a lot of tubes to fit inside your body!

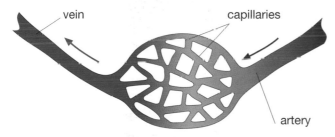

Figure 4 Blood flows from arteries into capillaries and then into veins.

Questions

2 Why do arteries need thick muscular walls?

3 Why does having thin walls help capillaries to do their job.

4 When we exercise we need to provide more oxygen to our muscles. Write a short paragraph about how our body does this. Use the following words in your answer

**lungs   oxygen   heart   pulse
breathing   faster**

Remember

Copy and complete the sentences. Use these words:

**arteries   capillaries   heart
blood vessels   veins**

Blood moves around in a system of tubes called **b**_____ **v**_____. The **h**_____ pumps blood around your body. Blood containing lots of oxygen moves away from your heart in tubes called **a**_____. Blood containing waste carbon dioxide moves back to your heart in **v**_____. Thin tubes called **c**_____ join arteries to veins.

How do the lungs work

Key words

alveoli Thin, damp air sacs in the lungs where gases are exchanged

bronchi The tubes that lead from the trachea into each lung

bronchioles Thinner tubes that branch throughout the lungs

trachea The wind pipe which carries air from the mouth and nose to the lungs

As you read this page you are probably breathing in about a mugful of air each minute. After running around for a couple of minutes this can increase 10 times to about 2.5 litres each minute. The amount of air we breathe in and out depends on what we are doing. The more active we are, the more oxygen we need. To get this oxygen we breathe faster and take more air in every breath so that more oxygen reaches deep into the lungs.

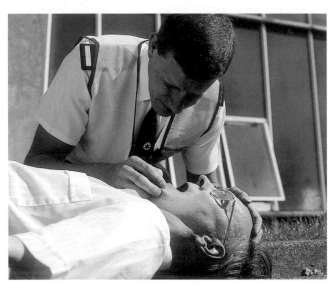

Figure 1 This person is being given mouth-to-mouth resuscitation because he has stopped breathing.

Questions

1 How many 'mugfuls' of air will you breathe during your science lesson today?

2 If a mugful of air is 0.25 litres, how many litres of air will you breathe during your science lesson today?

3 If your breathing rate didn't change during the day, how many litres of air would you breathe in 24 hours?

Most of the time we don't think about breathing. It's only when we are 'out of breath' that it becomes a problem. Healthy people breathe faster and deeper when they are exercising.

	Oxygen	Nitrogen	Carbon dioxide	Other gases
Air breathed in (inhaled air) %	21	78	0.04	0.96
Air breathed out (exhaled air) %	17	78	4	0.96

Table 1 The different gases in air

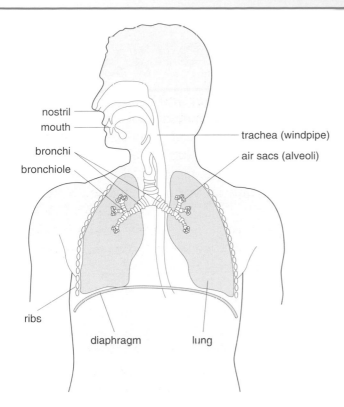

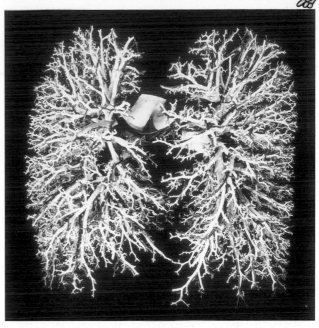

Figure 3 A model of the human lungs, showing the blood vessels (red) and air passages (white).

Figure 2 This shows how air passes through your nose down into the deepest part of your lungs.

We have to breathe in and out to stay alive. Air is breathed in through your nose and mouth, and then down air passages into two lungs, one on each side of your body. Figure 2 shows that air goes down a wide tube called the **trachea**, which splits into two branches called the **bronchi**. One of these goes into each lung. The bronchi divide into many smaller tubes called **bronchioles**. The bronchioles end in millions of tiny air sacs called **alveoli** (single: alveolus). Alveoli are like tiny, very thin, damp balloons at the end of each bronchi. If they were spread out flat they would cover a very large area – about the size of a tennis court. Blood flows around the alveoli in a web of capillaries.

Questions

Use Table 1 to answer the following questions

4 Which of the three main gases in air makes up most of the air that we breathe?

5 If 17% of the air we breathe out is oxygen, how much oxygen is transferred to our bloodstream through the lungs?

Remember

Write a short paragraph about the journey that oxygen takes to get from the air into our bloodstream. Use the following words:

nose bronchus trachea alveolus bloodstream bronchiole

Getting enough oxygen

asthma   A medical condition that affects the airways, making breathing more difficult

bronchitis   An infection of the air passages

inhaler   A device used by asthma sufferers to help them breathe more easily

Figure 1 Inhalers deliver liquid droplets of medicine to widen air passages by relaxing the muscle wall.

Not getting enough oxygen can have some very serious effects on your body.

People that suffer from **asthma** can be 'short of breath'. They often have to use an **inhaler**. Muscles in their air passages sometimes contract making the tubes much narrower. Imagine blowing down some tubes. As the tubes get narrower, it becomes more and more difficult to push the air down them. The chemicals in the inhaler relax the muscles, open up the air passages and allow the person to breathe more easily.

Sometimes air passages get infected and inflamed, causing **bronchitis**. People with bronchitis find it difficult to breathe and cough a lot. Their bronchial tubes are inflamed and lined with a sticky substance called mucus. Trying to cough up mucus can cause damage to the lungs.

Questions

1   If a part of the body has -itis at the end it means that that part is inflamed. Work out which part of the body is inflamed in the following medical conditions. (Have a look at the diagram on page 46 to help you!)
    a)   tracheitis
    b)   bronchiolitis
    c)   bronchitis

2   Why does making the air passages wider help people who suffer from asthma?

Figure 2 People with severe lung damage need to breathe air with extra oxygen in.

People who have a lot of difficulty breathing may have to breathe air that has a higher amount of oxygen in than normal, like the man in Figure 2.

What causes asthma?

Asthma can be caused by allergies to house dust mites (tiny creatures that live off house dust), cats, dogs, and mould. Being around all of these things can trigger an asthma attack.

Cigarette, cigar and pipe smoke can also give someone an asthma attack. Some people will have an asthma attack if they take aspirin. Even fairly simple things like being out in the cold air, exercising at school or when playing can cause attacks too. It has also been known for people to suffer an attack just from laughing. But people who suffer from asthma say that it is worse when they are worried.

Having asthma does not always mean that you have to give up the things that you like doing, such as sport. Paula Radcliffe, the long distance runner, has asthma but it didn't stop her being a world class athlete and winning a silver medal at the World Championships.

Questions

3   Name three things that can cause asthma.

4   Name three things, different from the things in Question 3, that can trigger an asthma attack.

5   Draw a poster to explain to a junior school pupil what asthma is and what causes and triggers it.

Remember

Copy and complete the sentences. Use these words (you can use the words more than once):

**faster   glucose   more   deeper
increases   energy**

During strenuous exercise, **m**_____ oxygen is needed to react with **g**_____ to release **e**_____ to make our muscles work efficiently. There is more carbon dioxide to be removed. To meet these needs we breathe **d**_____ and **f**_____ At the same time our heart rate **i**_____.

Figure 3 Paula Radcliffe won the silver medal for 10 000 metres at the World Championships in 1999.

Finishing off!

Make a table with two columns in your exercise book. Put the heading TRUE in one column and FALSE in the other. Now read the statements below and copy them into the correct column. If you think **a)** is false, put it into the false column, if you think it's true put it in the true column, and so on. Do it in pencil first, check your answers with your teacher and go over the correct ones in pen.

a) From your lungs, carbon dioxide is taken into the blood.

b) In lungs, the alveoli are surrounded by capillaries so that gases can easily pass between them.

c) Blood returns to the heart through veins.

d) Arteries have thicker walls than veins.

e) Blood being pumped to the tissues contains more oxygen than blood moving back to the heart.

f) Blocked arteries can cause a heart attack.

g) Veins carry blood that is rich in oxygen.

h) The heart has one pump.

i) During exercise the amount of air you breathe in goes down.

j) Blood is completely liquid.

k) The heart doesn't need a blood supply because it contains blood.

l) People who have asthma find it easy to breathe, people who do not have asthma need medicines to help them breathe.

Copy the two diagrams on this page carefully into your exercise book

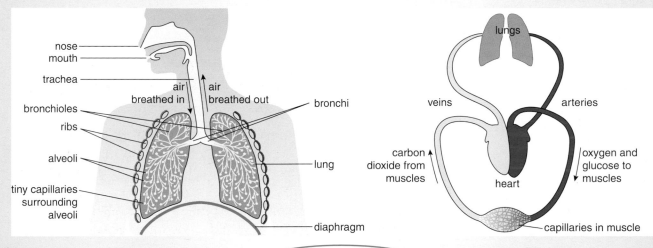

1 Take a new page in your exercise book. Make a list of all the key words in this chapter down the side. Take two lines per word. Try to write the meaning of each word without looking. Then go back and fill in any you did not know or got wrong. Now learn to spell them using the look–say–cover–write method.

Web sites to visit:

An on-line exploration of the heart
http://sln.fi.edu/biosci/biosci.html

CHAPTER 5

Reactions and mixtures

Phlogiston

Yes, this is made of water, air and fire

The Ancient Greeks thought there were only four pure substances: air, earth, fire and water. They thought wood was a mixture of water (from rain), fire (from sunlight) and air. When wood burned, the fire and air escaped. They thought iron was a mixture of earth and fire. When iron rusted the fire part escaped.

Three hundred years ago, scientists explained burning like this:

Wood contains **phlogiston**. When they burn they release the phlogiston – you can see the flames as it escapes. Air has no phlogiston in it so it does not burn. Iron releases its phlogiston slowly as it rusts.'

Iron gets heavier as it rusts. If the phlogiston idea was true, iron loses phlogiston as it rusts. This did not seem sensible.

The famous scientists **Joseph Priestley** and **Antoine Lavoisier** worked on this problem. Priestley made a gas. Things burned brightly in this gas. He did not realise he had made a new gas. It was Lavoisier who realised that it was different. He named it **oxygen**.

Oxygen is only one part of air – about one-fifth. Most of air is made up of a gas called **nitrogen**.

Sadly Lavoisier was executed in 1794, during the French Revolution. Priestley went on to invent fizzy drinks.

Activity

Turn this piece of science history into a poster. Use these words on your poster:

Ancient Greeks air phlogiston Priestley Lavoisier oxygen

Pure thoughts

harmful   A substance that will poison people and make them ill

molecule   One particle of a compound

pure substance   Contains only one type of particle

Pure substances contain only one sort of particle. This can be one atom or a small group of atoms called a **molecule**. To most people a pure substance means one that contains no **harmful** substances, such as pure orange juice.

Typical composition – mg/litre			
Calcium	35.0	Sulphate	6.0
Magnesium	15.0	Nitrate	1.5
Sodium	12.0	Fluoride	<0.2
Potassium	1.3	Iron	<0.03
Bicarbonate	179.0	Aluminium	<0.005
Chloride	10.0		

Total dry residue at 180°C – 186 mg/litre

Table 1   Ingredients label found on a bottle of *pure* mountain spring water

Look at the ingredients label for pure mountain spring water. It contains substances that have dissolved in the water as it flowed through the mountain rock. It's nearly pure water, but there are other particles in the mixture as well as water particles.

In science, pure means containing only one type of particle.

These are pure substances:

- pure water: contains only water particles
- copper metal: contains only copper particles
- sugar crystals: contain only sugar particles
- oxygen gas: contains only oxygen particles

Questions

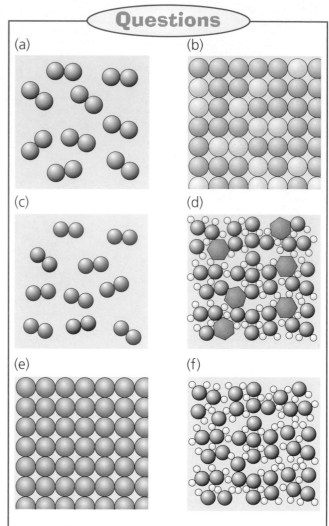

(a)   (b)   (c)   (d)   (e)   (f)

Look at the six boxes in the diagram above.

1 Which two are gases? (*Hint*: separate particles)

2 Which is pure oxygen?

3 Which is air? (*Hint*: oxygen and other gases mixed)

4 Which two are liquids? (*Hint*: jumble of particles touching each other)

5 Which is pure water? (*Hint*: made of molecules that are the same)

6 Which is sugar dissolved in water?

7 Which two diagrams show solid materials? (*Hint*: regular pattern of particles)

8 One is pure copper metal, the other is brass (*Hint*: brass is a mixture of copper and zinc). Which is pure copper and which is brass?

Useful mixtures

Nearly all the cooking we do makes mixtures. Mixtures can make very useful materials.

Mixtures often have very different properties from the pure substances that make them. All of the materials in Table 2 are mixtures. Some materials only work as mixtures.

Mixture	Made from...
black ink	several dyes and water
blood	red cells, white cells, salt and water
butter	milk fat, salt and water
glass	washing soda, sand and lead metal

Table 2

Questions

9 What do you mix to make a cup of coffee?

10 Describe a 'mix' that you have made to eat (a pizza topping or a sandwich) that is better than one food on its own. Explain why it is better.

Figure 1 This is what you need to make a cup of white coffee and a sponge cake.

Remember

mixtures   particle   pure   different

When we say something is **p____** we mean it doesn't harm people. But pure really means substances that contain only one type of **p_____**.

Many materials are **m_____**. These materials have **d_____** properties to the substances they are made from.

Into thin air

Key words

carbon dioxide   A gas made by burning and breathing, a compound

hurricane   A very strong wind storm

mass   How much there is of a material

photosynthesis   How a plant makes its own food.

Figure 2   Coal burns and disappears?

Coal is mainly carbon atoms. The carbon does not disappear when coal burns. It reacts with the oxygen in the air and makes **carbon dioxide**. This is a gas, so it mixes back into the air. The air gets heavier because carbon is added to it.

Figure 1   Damage caused by the 1999 hurricane.

Where does the push come from to flatten buildings and uproot trees during a **hurricane**? It comes from moving air.

During the hurricane in France in 1999 there was millions of pounds of damage done – all caused by thin air. In fact, thin air is not that thin. We're just used to it.

In the space under a normal two person school desk there is about 1 kg of air. A school hall contains about 6 tonnes of air. When these large lumps start moving about it's no wonder trees get pushed over.

Where the burning things go

In many chemical changes, substances gain or lose **mass**. Really the mass is being given to and got back from the air.

Figure 3   Trees appear from nowhere?

Trees take carbon dioxide out of the air. They use it to make wood. The gas is taken in by the leaves. Water is absorbed by the roots. **Photosynthesis** turns these two substances into wood.

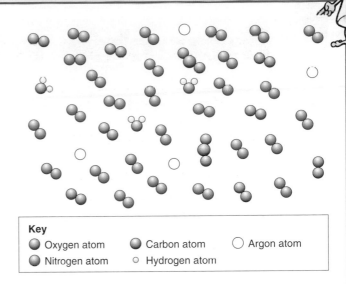

Key

⬤ Oxygen atom   ⬤ Carbon atom   ○ Argon atom
⬤ Nitrogen atom   ○ Hydrogen atom

Figure 4 Some of the gases in air are elements and some are compounds. Particle pictures of gases let us say which is which.

Investigating air

We often use the word 'pure' to describe clean air, but air is a mixture of several gases. All the gases in air are colourless and don't smell.

Gases in the air

Oxygen	21 %
Nitrogen	78 %
Carbon dioxide	0.03 %
Noble gases (mainly argon)	approx. 1%
Water vapour	a varying amount depending on the weather

Table 1 Gases in the air

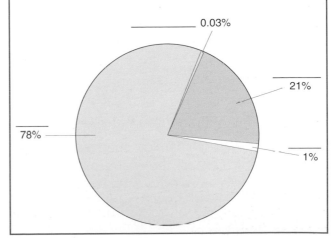

Strange reactions – no!

Key words

combustion   Burning to release energy

displacement   One substance 'pushes' another out of a compound

oxidation   Combining with oxygen atoms

precipitation   A solid is made when fluids are mixed

predictable   Always happens in the same way

thermal decomposition   Molecules fall apart on heating to make simpler molecules

Figure 2   The oxidation of magnesium.

There are lots of types of chemical reaction. Here we will meet six of them.

Oxidation

Metals react with oxygen in the air. They make new substances called oxides. Magnesium burns and makes magnesium oxide. This is a white powder. Adding oxygen to a substance is called **oxidation**.

Combustion

Combustion is a special sort of oxidation reaction. Oxygen in the air is used to burn a fuel and transfer energy as heat and light.

Thermal decomposition

Figure 3

Lots of substances fall apart when heated. This is called **thermal decomposition**. Your breakfast toast is made like this. Some of the starch particles in the bread make the brown toasty colour. So you get a nice texture and a stronger taste.

Figure 1

Strike a match,
light the gas cooker,
cook a fried egg,
digest the food,
then use the energy you get to play tennis.

All five of these use chemical changes to make them work. We expect the changes in matches, gas and eggs to work every time we try them. Chemical changes are **predictable** – they always happen the same way.

Precipitation

Figure 4 This pupil is demonstrating a precipitation reaction.

When you bubble colourless carbon dioxide gas through colourless lime water solution, they react and an insoluble substance is made. The insoluble substance makes the liquid cloudy. It is called a **precipitate**.

Displacement

Figure 5 A stealth bomber – a high performance aeroplane.

Titanium is used for aeroplanes. Titanium ore is turned into metal by using sodium metal. The sodium steals, or **displaces**, the oxygen from the titanium ore, leaving useful titanium metal.

Fizz reactions

Figure 6 A fizz reaction.

Figure 6 shows acid and sodium hydrogen carbonate being mixed. It makes lots of fizz by giving off carbon dioxide gas. When you cook scones this reaction is used to make the scones

Remember

The word 'thermal' means to do with heating.

What are these words that are also to do with heating?

Copy and complete the sentences.

Therm__: a type of underwear to keep you warm.

Therm_____: used to measure temperature.

Therm__ fla__: keeps drinks hot.

Therm_____: keeps the room the same temperature.

Make a list of other words you can think of that begin with 'therm-' and write down their meanings. Use a dictionary. Are there any that are *not* to do with heating.

Questions

Write down the type of reaction in each of these examples:

1 Making charcoal by heating wood.

2 Petrol burns in a car engine to release heat.

3 Milk goes sour as it reacts with oxygen in the air.

4 Limestone rock makes bubbles when vinegar is put on it.

5 Baked potatoes in the oven go crispy and dark on the outside.

6 When an iron nail is put in copper sulphate solution, copper metal gets deposited on the surface of the iron nail. Iron particles take the place of the copper in the solution.

It's frighteningly tiny

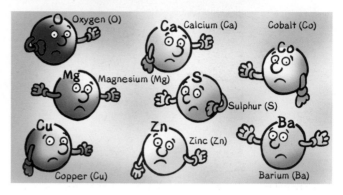

Figure 2 These atoms are a bit less brave. They have two hands.

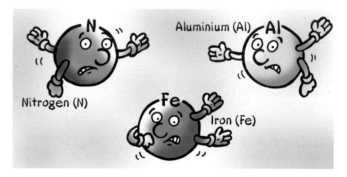

Figure 3 Some atoms have three hands. They still need all their hands held. They are scaredy.

Figure 4 But the scaredyest of all is this one. Carbon is special. It is very keen to hold onto its mates. That's why pure carbon – diamond – is so hard. It links up in long chains to make really big groups. It is the only atom that does this.

Key words

electrons Tiny particles that orbit round the outside of atoms

valency Number of 'links' that one atom makes with other atoms

Atoms are simple creatures. They have only one wish in the world. They want to have their outer shell full of **electrons**.

Atoms are very small. Very small indeed. In fact *incredibly* small. So small that you can't see them, even with a microscope. Because they are small they are frightened. Can you remember when you were small and went out into crowded places? You kept close together with your friends and held hands. You have two hands. You felt safe if both hands were held. Atoms are the same. They are 'safe' only if all their hands are being held. But atoms have different numbers of hands. The bravest have only one hand. Here are pictures of some of them.

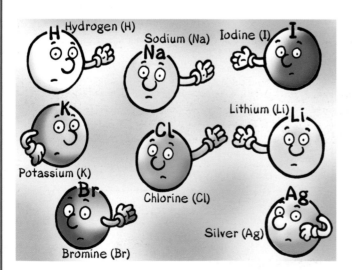

Figure 1 The bravest atoms.

When atoms hold hands with their friends they are happy. They say to each other 'We have reacted. We are safe from change for a while.'

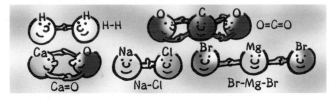

Figure 5 No free hands.

The atoms in Figure 5 have joined together. We say they have 'reacted.' They now feel safe. What nice groups. Each group is a molecule. It has no free hands so it cannot react any more.

These groups are content. They have all their hands held and feel less small. They are molecules, made up from small groups of atoms.

Figure 6 No molecules for these atoms.

Strangest of all, there are some 'dead tough' atoms. They stay on their own all the time. They have no hands at all to hold on to other atoms. They are real loners; they form no compounds at all.

Of course, this is only a story to help you understand. The atoms do form small groups. And with the number of 'friends' you have met here. The number of hands is called the **valency**. Make sure you know the number of 'hands' for each atom.

Questions

Now see if you can draw these groups:

1   One atom of carbon being friendly with hydrogen.

2   Nitrogen being friendly with hydrogen.

3   Sodium being friendly with oxygen.

4   Aluminium being friendly with chlorine.

5   Magnesium being friendly with oxygen.

6   Chlorine on its own has a formula of Cl_2. Why do these atoms go round in pairs?

Remember

Copy and fill in this table. Put all the elements mentioned in the questions and text in the correct column.

Zero hands so makes no links with other atoms	One hand so makes one link with other atoms	Two hands so makes two links with other atoms	Three hands so makes three links with other atoms	Four hands so makes four links with other atoms
(4 elements)	(8 elements)	(8 elements)	(3 elements)	(1 element)

Always the same recipe

Key words

chemical formula A short way of writing the ratio of one atom to another

combine Join together

ingredients The things a cook uses to make a cake

ratio The number of one type of atom there is compared to the number of other atoms

Figure 1 These identical cakes have been made by a trained cook.

Cooking and chemistry can have pleasing results. Both have rules about how much of one material will combine with another. If you follow them correctly, the results are predictable. Cooks **combine** exactly the right quantities of different **ingredients**. The fat combines with exactly the right amount of flour so the pastry tastes good.

When chemicals react, they follow rules about how much of one element will combine with another. Even when chemicals fall apart, they follow the same strict rules. The atoms react so that all their hands are still held.

One oxygen particle combines with two lithium particles to make one lithium oxide.

Lithium oxide

Three oxygen particles combine with six lithium particles to make three lithium oxides.

You can see the **ratio** of lithium atoms to oxygen atoms stays the same no matter how many 'particles' of lithium oxide are made. There are always two lithium atoms for every one oxygen atom.

One copper carbonate splits up into one copper oxide and one carbon dioxide particle.

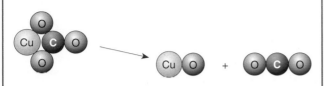

Five copper carbonates split up into five copper oxides and five carbon dioxide molecules.

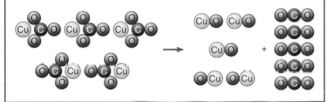

When green copper carbonate is heated it decomposes. Copper oxide is left and carbon dioxide gas is given off.

The ratio of the number of one atom to another always stays the same. This can be written as the **chemical formula**:

Li_2O: 2 lithium to 1 oxygen

CuO: 1 copper (Cu) to 1 oxygen

CO_2: 1 carbon to 2 oxygens

$CuCO_3$: 1 copper (Cu) to 1 carbon to 3 oxygens.

Questions

1 How many atoms of oxygen are there in an oxygen molecule?

2 If 400 lithium atoms were combined with oxygen, how many oxygen particles would be needed?

3 How many oxygen *molecules* is this?

Remember

Copy and complete the sentences. Use these words:

formula   compound   join

Atoms **j**____ together in a fixed ratio. The chemical **f**_____ show the ratio of atoms in the **c**_____.

Finishing off!

Brainwaves

Can you understand all the links on the mind map? Copy the mind map onto a double-page spread in your book or onto A3 paper. Make any changes you think are needed. Add extra pictures to make it clearer to you.

Or as a class task, divide into groups and take a section of the mind map. Produce a big display of the map.

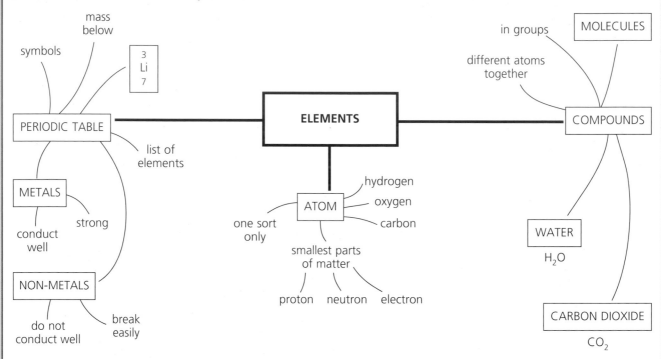

Questions

1   Take a new page in your exercise book. Make a list of all the Key Words from the boxes in this chapter down the side. Take two lines per word. Try to write the meaning of each word without looking. Then go back and fill in any you did not know or got wrong

Now learn to spell them by the look–say–cover–write method.

2   Imagine that a new element, Hoddium, has been discovered.
a)   What would it look like if it were a metal?
b)   How would you test Hoddium to see if it was a metal?

Web sites to visit:

Making Compounds
http://www.geocities.com/CapeCanaveral/Hangar/3296/makingcompounds.html

Magnetism

Starter Activity
Action at a distance

Some things only happen in stories – like being able to make someone float in mid air like in the picture below. Action at a distance: is it magic or fact?

If you jump out of an aeroplane, you'll find that the Earth will attract you downwards. Its force of attraction will pull you down without touching you. (It doesn't touch you until the *end* of your fall!) This is called gravity.

A magnet can also exert a force on another magnet without touching it. **Magnetism** and **gravity** can act at a distance.

These forces have strength and direction. Gravity acts towards the centre of the Earth. Magnetism acts towards and away from the poles of a magnet. You can draw lines or use iron filings to help you understand about the lines of force around a magnet.

Some things only happen in stories.

Questions

1 Write down the things that you know about the force of gravity and the force of magnetism that are:
   a) the same
   b) different.

2 What can we use magnets for?

3 Why would a compass be of no use if you were trying to find your way around space?

Magnetic forces

Key words

compass A small magnet that always points from South to North

field lines Lines used to represent a magnetic field. They are also called lines of force

magnetic field The space around a magnet where its force can act.

Magnets can attract and repel

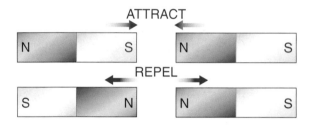

Figure 1 Magnets can attract and repel each other.

Magnets are fun. You can stick them on the fridge. You can put them together – sometimes they attract and sometimes they repel. They push and pull each other without touching. The force of magnetism acts at a distance. The space around a magnet where its force can act is called its **magnetic field**.

Questions

1 Which word means the opposite of attract?

2 What is the name of the space around a magnet in which its force can act?

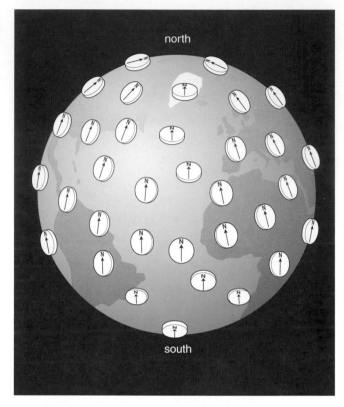

Figure 2 Compasses all over the Earth point northwards.

The Earth itself is a very large magnet. If you hang a magnet up so that it is free to swing, it will always settle in the same direction. One end will point towards the North and the other end will point to the South. Chinese sailors discovered this a long time ago. They invented the **compass**.

A compass

A compass is a small magnet that can swing freely. Compasses all over the Earth will always point from South to North. So wherever you are, a compass will tell you which way is North and which way is South. The end of a compass or magnet that points north is called its North pole. The end that points south is called its South pole.

You can use little compasses to trace the patterns of magnetic forces that act in the area around a magnet. You get a pattern of lines in loops. These are called **field lines**, or sometimes lines of force. Arrows on the lines show which way the compass needle points. The lines always go from the North pole of the magnet to the South pole of the magnet.

Figure 3 Walkers use a map and a compass to guide them home.

Field lines

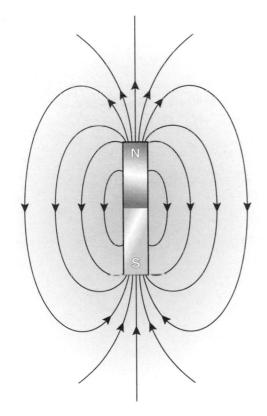
Figure 4 The pattern of field lines around a magnet.

Questions

3 Why is it useful that the Earth is a magnet?

4 Copy and complete this diagram to show the complete pattern of field lines. Mark the North pole of the magnet with an N.

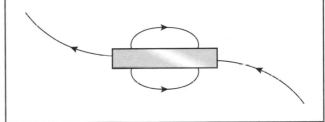

Remember

Copy and complete the sentences. Use these words:

**North   field   distance   attract
magnetic   force   magnet**

Magnetic force can act at a **d**_____. The space round a magnet where it can exert force is called its magnetic **f**_____. The Earth acts as a large **m**_____ and exerts forces on other magnets. Every magnet has a **N**_____ pole and a South pole. Magnets can **a**_____ or repel each other. Lines of **f**_____ are also called field lines. They show the direction of the magnetic force that can act at different places in a **m**_____ field.

6.2

Patterns of magnetism

Key words

electromagnet   A magnet made by an electric current flowing in a coil of wire

magnetic   Describes a material that is attracted by a magnet

Iron and steel are the most common magnetic materials. If you hold a piece of iron or steel next to a magnet, it will feel a force. Steel is good for making permanent bar magnets because steel magnets keep their magnetism. Compass needles are made of steel.

Attracting and repelling

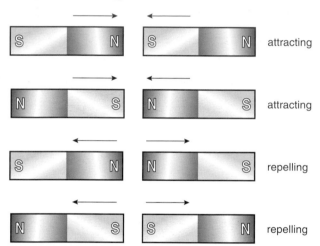

Figure 1 Two different poles attract, two poles that are the same repel.

If you hold two strong magnets close together, sometimes you will feel them attracting each other and sometimes they will repel each other (push each other away).

There is a pattern to the pushing and pulling. North poles attract South poles and South poles attract North poles. Two poles that are *different* always *attract* each other. Two poles that are the *same* always *repel* each other.

Magnetic materials

Most materials aren't **magnetic**. When you hold just one magnet, your hand can't feel any force. Your hand is not made of magnetic material.

Questions

1   What effect does:
a)   a North pole of a magnet have on another North pole?
b)   a North pole of a magnet have on a South pole?

2   Why is steel good for making compass needles?

Electromagnets

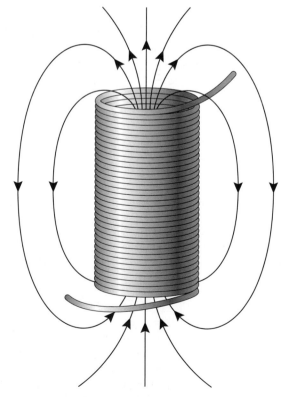

Figure 2 An electromagnet is a coil with an electric current. It has a pattern of field lines around it.

66

When an electric current flows in a wire, the space around the wire becomes a magnetic field. The electric current creates magnetism.

If a wire in an electric circuit is made into a tight coil, the magnetism of each turn of the coil adds to the total strength of the magnetic field. A coil makes a strong magnet that can be switched on and off. It is called an **electromagnet**.

Look at the patterns of field lines around the electromagnet.

- The lines are closer together where the field is stronger.

- The lines and arrows show the direction of the force of the field.

Remember: These lines are imaginary. They are just a useful way to show the force field round the magnet.

Questions

3   In what ways is an electromagnet more useful than a permanent magnet?

4   Name one use for electromagnets.

Remember

Copy and complete the sentences. Use these words:

**permanent   same   switched
electromagnets   attract**

Poles that are different always **a**_____. Poles that are the **s**_____ always repel. Most materials are no good for making magnets. Steel is useful for making **p**_____ magnets. **E**_____ are coils of wire. Their magnetism can be **s**_____ on and off.

Figure 3 A strong electromagnet is used to lift pieces of steel in this scrapyard.

Power lines

When a current flows in a wire there is a magnetic field around the wire.

Figure 1

TV presenter: Here in the village of Aberffordd the local doctor, Dr Roberts has warned us about a very high rate of cancer. Dr Roberts, is this unusual?

Doctor Roberts: Everybody knows that cancer is a common disease, but here in Aberffordd it's more than three times as common as the average for the whole of the UK.

TV presenter: So what can be the cause of this?

Doctor Roberts: We don't know. We've tested the water and that's completely normal. Many people here work on farms and it could

be that some of the **pesticides** they use have harmful effects. But in similar farming villages there isn't the same high rate of cancer. One suggestion is that the problem is caused by the high voltage power cables that pass over the village from the power station two miles away.

TV presenter: They look like ordinary power cables to me.

Doctor Roberts: Yes, but all power cables carry a strong electric current, and that means that there are strong magnetic fields all around them.

TV presenter: Are you saying that the magnetic fields in the space around the cables are causing cancer?

Doctor Roberts: We can't say for sure, and the electricity company say there's no evidence that magnetism causes cancer. But that doesn't stop people worrying.

TV presenter: Is there anything about these particular magnetic fields that could be a problem?

Doctor Roberts: Well the current in the cables is large, and that makes strong magnetic effects. Also the current isn't steady. It vibrates backwards and forwards 50 times a second. It's **alternating current**. That means that the magnetic fields are also vibrating. Perhaps the vibrations can affect the chemistry in a human body.

TV presenter: Also with me is Nigel Morris who works for the electricity company. He's the man responsible for operating these cables. Mr Morris, are your power cables making people ill, and causing some of them to die?

Nigel Morris: Over many years we've made detailed studies on possible effects of power cables. There's simply no known way in which the magnetic fields in the space around power cables can cause cancer. The situation in Aberffordd is a mystery to everybody, but I'm absolutely confident that our power cables are not causing the problem.

TV presenter: There is a problem here in Aberffordd, but nobody has any ideas about the cause, and still less about what can be done. This is Gita Patel, News at Nine, Aberffordd.

Every wire which carries an electric current has a magnetic field around it. You can use a compass to follow the pattern of the magnetic field lines as in Figure 2. These lines show the direction of the magnetic force. The bigger the current, the stronger the magnetic field. If the current varies, the strength of the magnetic field varies in just the same way.

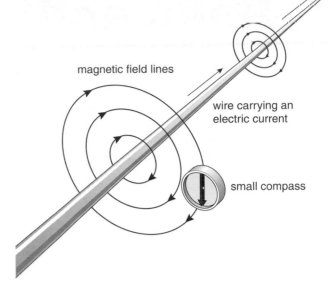

Figure 2 A compass will line up with the magnetic field around a wire that has an electric current flowing through it.

Questions

1 Why is it unlikely that the problem at Aberffordd is caused by:
   a) the water supply?
   b) pesticides from farms?

2 Why are the magnetic fields around power lines strong?

3 As far as we know, magnetic fields are harmless. What research could scientists do to try to find out more about this?

Remember

Copy and complete the sentences. Use these words:

lines   magnetic   current   electric

There is always a **m**_____ field around a wire when it is carrying an **e**_____ current. The bigger the **c**_____ in the wire, the stronger the magnet. A pattern of field **l**_____ shows the direction of the magnetic forces.

Bells and relays

The electric bell

An electric bell is an electromagnetic device. It uses an electric current to create a magnetic field. Magnetic forces make the hammer move to hit the gong.

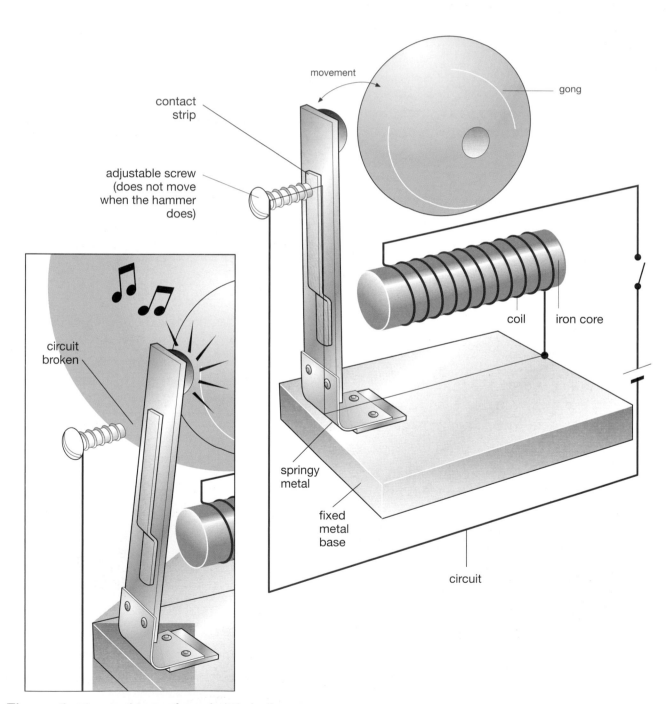

movement

gong

contact strip

adjustable screw (does not move when the hammer does)

coil   iron core

circuit broken

springy metal

fixed metal base

circuit

Figure 1 The workings of an electric bell.

The electromagnet in an electric bell is a coil of wire. It is wound round an iron rod (core). When the current flows, the iron makes the magnetism very strong. When the current is switched off, the magnetism fades very quickly.

The coil exerts a magnetic force of attraction on the iron hammer. It can bend on its support and it moves over to hit the gong. As it moves, the contact strip moves with it. The strip moves away from the fixed adjustable screw. The screw and the contact strip are like a switch in the circuit. So when the hammer hits the gong, the circuit is broken. The current then stops, the coil loses its magnetism and the hammer bends back. The contact strip touches the screw again and makes contact, a current flows and its magnetic field attracts the hammer which strikes the gong again.

The hammer dashes backwards and forwards several times a second. Each time it hits the gong there is another ringing sound.

Questions

1 In an electric bell
   a) Why does the hammer move towards the gong?
   b) Why does it move away again?
   c) What is the iron core for?

Electromagnetic relay

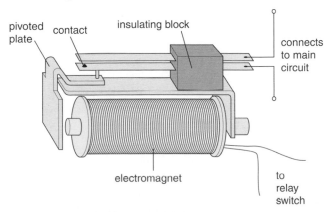

pivoted plate   contact   insulating block

connects to main circuit

electromagnet

to relay switch

Figure 2 An electromagnetic relay.

You may have heard a remote click or clunk when the central heating or washing machine turns on. This is usually a sign that an **electromagnetic relay** is switching on part of a circuit.

A relay is an electromagnetic switch. It has a coil of wire wound on an iron core. When a current flows through the coil, it makes the iron core into an electromagnet. The electromagnet attracts the pivoted plate. As it moves it pushes the switch contacts together, switching on the main circuit.

With an electromagnetic relay, a small current can be made to switch on a very large current.

Car starter motors need a relay to switch them on. The ignition key inside the car switches on the relay. A small current of less than 1 amp closes the relay contacts to switch on the starter motor. The motor needs 50 or 60 amps to start the engine.

Questions

2 Name two places in your home where you might find an electromagnetic relay.

3 What is the main advantage of an electromagnetic relay?

Remember

Copy and complete the sentences. Use these words:

lose   hammer   on   adjustable electromagnet   contact strip repeats   current

An electric bell works by using a coil as an **e**_____. The electric **c**_____ in the coil makes it magnetic, so that it attracts the **h**_____. The hammer hits the gong. The movement breaks the circuit between the metal **c**_____ **s**_____ and the **a**_____ screw. That makes the coil **l**_____ its magnetism. The hammer moves back, switching the circuit back **o**_____ again. The process **r**_____ itself many times every second.

Loudspeakers

Key words

amplifier   An electronic device used to increase the loudness of sound signals

loudspeaker   A device which transfers electrical energy to sound energy

Loudspeakers

The metal strings of the electric guitar in Figure 1 do not make a very loud sound. To make the sounds loud enough to be heard, the vibrations of the string generate electric currents in the guitar's circuit. These electric currents are quite weak. They flow into an **amplifier**, which makes bigger currents with the same patterns in them. The bigger currents pass into the **loudspeaker** which vibrates with the same pattern, but is much louder.

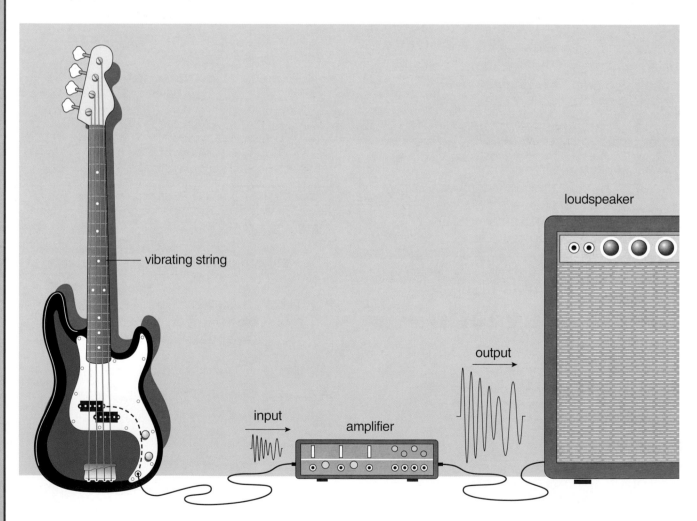

loudspeaker

vibrating string

input

amplifier

output

Figure 1   The patterns of vibration of the guitar string make patterns in the electric current in the guitar's electric circuits. The current passes through an amplifier which makes a bigger current with the same pattern. The amplified current passes through the coil in a loudspeaker. The loudspeaker vibrates. The sound that travels through the air carries the same patterns as the sound make by the guitar string but now it is LOUDER.

Now the quiet guitar is as loud as you want it to be. The process of making loud sounds from quiet ones is called amplification.

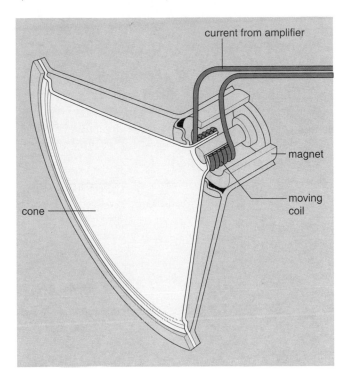

Figure 2 In a loudspeaker, a changing magnetic force creates vibration of the coil and the cone.

The main part of the loudspeaker is a cone of card or other stiff material fixed to a coil of wire which can slide over a fixed magnet. The changing electric currents from the amplifier flow through the coil. The coil becomes magnetic. That creates force between the coil and the fixed magnet. The pattern in the electric currents makes the force stronger and weaker, varying rapidly. The coil moves backwards and forwards rapidly pushing the cone and the surrounding air with it. So it makes a sound just like the guitar strings, but very much louder.

Questions

1 What does an amplifier do?

2 Describe what each of these does to make a loudspeaker produce sound:

amplifier   coil   fixed magnet   cone

Remember

Copy and complete the sentences. Use these words:

**amplifier   magnet   cone   magnetic
current   loudspeaker**

When an electric **c**_____ flows in a coil, the coil becomes **m**_____. A varying current in the coil of a **l**_____ creates a varying force between the coil and the fixed **m**_____. The varying current makes the coil vibrate. So the **c**_____ of the loudspeaker vibrates. It can make loud sounds. An **a**_____ takes the small electric current from a guitar pick-up and creates bigger currents that are strong enough to drive a loudspeaker.

Finishing off!

★ Every magnet has a North pole and a South pole. Poles that are different attract and poles that are the same repel.

★ The space around a magnet where it can exert a force is called its **magnetic field**.

★ **Field lines** show the direction of the magnetic force.

★ There is always a magnetic field around a wire when it is carrying an electric current.

★ A magnet made from a coil of wire is called an **electromagnet**.

★ An electromagnet is only magnetic when current flows through the coil. The magnetism can be switched on and off.

★ **Loudspeakers** are sources of sound. The vibrations of the loudspeaker are caused by a changing force between the electromagnet and a permanent magnet.

Questions

1 Take a new page in your exercise book. Make a list of all the Key Words from the boxes in this chapter down the side. Take two lines per word. Try to write the meaning of each word without looking. Then go back and fill in any you did not know or got wrong.

Now learn to spell them by the look–say–cover–write method.

2 Make a sketch of the pattern of magnetic field lines around
   a) a permanent magnet
   b) an electromagnet.

3 Describe the magnetic force between each of these pairs. Use the words *attract* or *repel*.
   a) Two North poles of a magnet.

   b) Two South poles of a magnet.
   c) A North pole and a South pole.
   d) A North pole and an unmagnetised piece of steel.
   e) A North pole of a permanent magnet and a North pole of an electromagnet.

4 Which of these use electromagnets to make sound?

   human voice   TV   radio   piano electric bell

5 Explain how magnets are used to sort cans of different metals for recycling.

6 Explain how an electric bell rings continuously and doesn't make just a single 'ding' of the hammer on the gong.

Web sites to visit:

Magnetism
   http://www.duboismarketing.com/magnetism.html

Explanation of magnetism
   http://www.school-for-champions.com/science/magnetism.htm

Micro-organisms and disease

Have you been ill recently? Perhaps you've had a cough or a cold. You might have had something more serious like chickenpox or measles. Most of the illnesses we have are not dangerous, but some can make you very sick, even kill you. In this chapter we will look at what causes illness and how we can try to prevent people from becoming ill.

Look at the picture on this page. What is the doctor checking on the patient? Can you name the instruments that the doctor is using to check the boy's temperature and heart rate? Think about any visits you have made to the doctor. What sort of questions did they ask you and what sort of tests did they carry out?

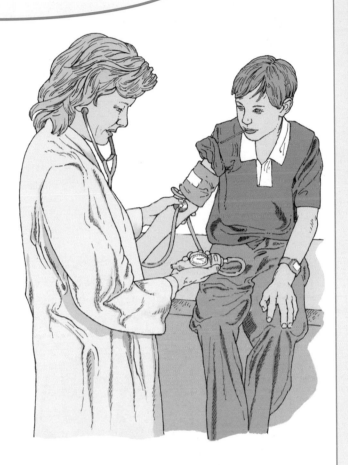

Questions

1 When you put your finger on your wrist, you can feel your pulse. What is your pulse and where does it come from?

2 If you get ill you begin to feel differently from the way you feel normally. Describe how the following illnesses feel:
   a) the common cold

   b) food poisoning
   c) the 'flu (influenza)
   d) a throat infection.

3 Gardeners often get cuts on their hands. Explain why it is important to cover a cut with sticking plaster, no matter how small the cut.

Microbes

What is a germ?

What we commonly call germs are in fact **micro-organisms**, like **bacteria** and **viruses**.

Figure 1

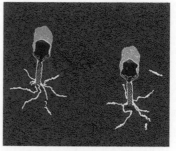

a) This virus is sitting on a bacterium. It uses the bacterium to reproduce, eventually killing it.

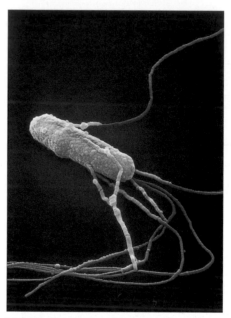

b) This bacterium is called salmonella, and it is the most common cause of food poisoning.

Figure 2

Micro-organisms are living things that are too small to see without a microscope. Not all micro-organisms are harmful. Some are useful to us.

There are millions of different types of bacteria. There are also many different types of virus.

If you compare a bacterium to a virus there are a number of differences. If you look at the photos in Figure 2 you can see that a bacterium is much bigger than a virus. Many bacteria are involved in the rotting of dead plants and animals. They feed off the dead plants and animals.

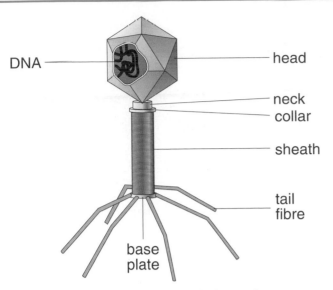

DNA — head

neck
collar

sheath

tail
fibre

base
plate

Figure 3 A virus which attacks bacteria.

A virus can exist for thousands of years unchanged and inactive. It doesn't need to feed off living or dead material. Once it finds a new cell to live in it can become active again. Figure 3 shows a labelled diagram of a virus.

Because micro-organisms are so small they can spread easily. There is an old saying 'coughs and sneezes spread diseases'.

Figure 4 A single sneeze produces a jet of water droplets that could spread the 'flu virus.

If you look at the photo of the person sneezing in Figure 4, you can see tiny water droplets spraying out from her nose and mouth. These droplets can contain millions of bacteria or viruses. The water spray doesn't immediately fall to the ground, so anyone breathing the droplets in can become infected. Lots of diseases can be spread this way, especially colds and 'flu.

When we get a high temperature, our body is trying to kill off the bacteria. Bacteria do not like very high temperatures. It stops them from reproducing.

Questions

1 Why should you sneeze and cough into a handkerchief?

2 How could a sneeze pass a cold from one person to another?

3 When we catch a cold we often begin sneezing and get a high temperature, what is the body trying to do when we sneeze and when our body heats up?

4 Bacteria are involved in the rotting of dead plants and animals. Why are bacteria involved in this and not viruses?

Remember

Copy and complete the sentences. Use these words:

**small   viruses   micro-organisms
bacteria**

B_____ and viruses are **m**_____. They are so **s**_____ they can't be seen without a microscope. Bacteria and **v**_____ are the cause of disease.

More micro-organisms

fungus A type of mould that lives in dark, warm, damp places

inflammation When part of your body becomes red and swollen

penicillin A type of fungus used to treat bacterial infections

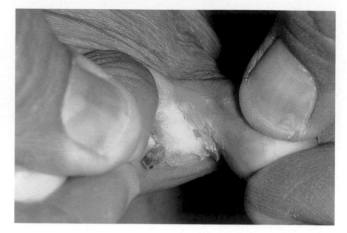

Figure 3 Athlete's foot.

Figure 1 Yeast has helped the bread to rise.

Yeast is a type of **fungus**. Athlete's foot is caused by a fungus. A fungus is a type of mould that lives in dark, warm, moist areas. On feet, it can grow between the toes or on the toes. It can also grow on the sole of the foot and on the toenails. Athlete's foot is often spread in places where people go barefoot such as public showers or swimming pools. It can cause painful **inflammation** and blisters if it is not treated. It usually starts with mild itching between the toes or on the arch of the foot and may spread to the bottom and sides of the foot.

Figure 2 The alcohol in this beer was produced by yeast.

Some micro-organisms like yeast can be helpful. As yeast grows it produces two waste products, the gas carbon dioxide and alcohol. We can use the carbon dioxide when baking bread to make the dough rise and to give the bread a light fluffy texture. When we brew beers, wines or spirits, yeast produces the alcohol in the drinks.

1 Yeast is a type of fungus used in baking and brewing. What other type of fungus is often used in cooking?

2 Athlete's foot is another type of fungus. What living conditions do both yeast and athlete's foot like?

3 Why is athlete's foot more likely to grow between your toes than on the top of your foot?

4 Why do swimming baths often make you go through a foot bath before you get into the pool?

How to avoid athlete's foot

- Wash your feet every day.
- Do not wear tight footwear, especially in the summer.
- Wear sandals in warm weather.
- Wear cotton socks and change them daily or more often if they become damp.
- Don't wear socks made of materials like nylon.
- If possible, go barefoot at home.
- Dust an anti-fungal powder into your shoes in the summertime.
- Always dry your feet after you have a bath or shower.
- Make sure to dry between your toes.
- Use foot powders to absorb moisture and kill any fungus.

Penicillin: a modern miracle

Some types of micro-organisms can protect us and keep us healthy. One type of mould that commonly grows on stale bread is penicillin. Penicillin is still used today to treat bacterial infections.

Penicillin was discovered by accident in 1928. Alexander Fleming was working in his laboratory when he noticed that bacteria close to where penicillin was growing were killed. Unfortunately Fleming couldn't work out how to produce lots of penicillin. Two other scientists, Howard Florey and Ernst Chain, managed to do this in the 1940s.

The first human to be treated with penicillin was Albert Alexander, a policeman who was dying from a serious bacterial infection. After being given penicillin his condition improved, but supplies of the drug ran out and he eventually died.

Penicillin saved many soldiers' lives during the war. In 1945 Fleming, Florey and Chain were all awarded the Nobel Prize for medicine.

Figure 4 Alexander Fleming

Figure 5 Howard Florey

Figure 6 Ernst Chain

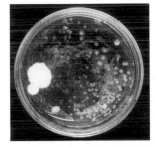

Figure 7 The penicillin (white) growing on a plate of bacteria

Question

5 How do you think the penicillin helped to save many soldiers' lives during the Second World War?

Remember

To help you remember what athlete's foot is and how to prevent it, produce a leaflet that could be given to swimmers at your local swimming pool warning about athlete's foot. Give them some advice on how to prevent it.

Spreading disease

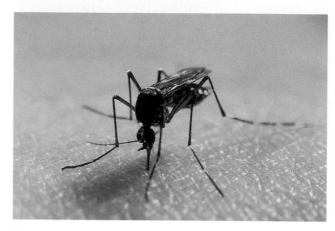

Figure 1 Mosquitoes spread malaria

Coughs and sneezes may spread diseases but just how do you catch them? Table 1 shows you some common diseases. It tells you how they are spread between people and how your body tries to protect you from the disease. There are a number of different ways that diseases can be spread.

1 **Person-to-person:** Bacteria and/or viruses are carried in blood or saliva. Some very **contagious** (easily caught) diseases are carried through the air.

2 **Food-borne infection**: Bacteria can **contaminate** food and may survive when it is heated. If the food is cooled and then reheated, the bacteria may grow and produce a poison that makes you vomit.

3 **Water-borne infection**: Contaminated water spreads diseases such as typhoid, cholera, dysentery and polio.

4 **Air-borne infection**: Bacteria and viruses can travel through the air in tiny droplets of water. This is what happens when someone coughs or sneezes.

5 **Insect-borne infection**: Many diseases are spread by insects. The plague was carried by rat fleas.

Questions

1 Look at Table 1. Which diseases cannot be treated easily?

2 Colds and 'flu are more common in the winter than in the summer. Being cold doesn't mean that you will catch a cold. Why are people more likely to catch colds in the winter? (*Hint*: think about how people behave in the winter months.)

3 Water-borne diseases are much more common in third world countries. Why do you think this is?

4 Most people confuse a common cold with 'flu. What are the similarities and differences between a cold and 'flu?

5 What should be done to prevent the spread of food poisoning? (*Hint*: Think of things you may have covered in food technology.)

Type of illness	What causes it?	How is it spread?	What are the symptoms?	How is it treated?
Sore throat	Bacteria	From person to person, by kissing or coughing	Sore throat	No treatment is normally given. The body kills the bacteria
Meningitis	Bacteria	Most people have the bacteria but do not get ill. It can be spread by coughing and kissing	Fever, severe headache, feeling sick and vomiting, stiff neck, dislike of bright lights	Injections or tablets. **Bacterial meningitis is very serious and must be treated immediately**
Food poisoning	Bacteria	By eating infected food that hasn't been cooked properly	Headache, stomach pain, diarrhoea, sometimes shivering and fever	Medicines are given only if the bacteria is thought to have spread to the blood
Common cold	Caused by over 200 different viruses	From person to person by coughing, sneezing, kissing or in crowds	Sore throat, runny nose, coughs and sneezes	No treatment, only relief from the symptoms
Influenza ('flu)	Virus	Airborne droplets from coughing and sneezing, also kissing	Fever, chills, aching joints and muscles, sore throat, runny nose. Usually much more intense than a cold and sufferers need to spend time recovering in bed	No treatment, only relief from the symptoms
Measles	Measles virus	Airborne droplets	Fever, rash, cold-like symptoms	No treatment, only relief from the symptoms
Chickenpox	Chickenpox virus	Airborne droplets or by direct contact with infected people	Slight fever, rash that develops into sores and blisters	No treatment, only relief from the symptoms

Table 1 Some common diseases

Remember

Copy and complete the sentences. Use these words:

insect   viruses   person   bacteria   contaminated

Diseases can be spread in 5 different ways:

1 From person to **p**_____.
2 By eating food contaminated by **b**_____.
3 By drinking **c**_____ water.
4 Being bitten by an **i**_____.
5 Breathing in bacteria or **v**_____.

Internal army

Key words

antibodies   Chemicals produced by white blood cells to protect us from infection

bone marrow   The jelly-like centre of a bone where blood cells are made

infection   When bacteria or viruses enter your body

lymph system   A system of tubes in the body containing a liquid which carries white blood cells

platelets   Parts of cells found in blood that help it to clot

white blood cells   The cells in our blood that fight disease

There are lots of things that can make us ill. Our bodies can fight off a lot of diseases. We have special organs and cells in our bodies that help to protect us and fight off disease.

Question

1   Look at Figure 1. Make a list of the organs and glands in the body that are there to try and protect you from disease.

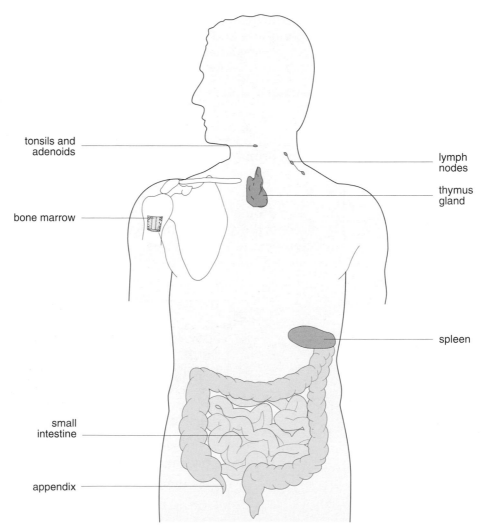

Figure 1 Disease-fighting organs and glands

Soldier cells

Blood is a sticky red liquid. It is probably the most important liquid in our bodies besides water. Almost half of our blood is made up of cells: red blood cells, **white blood cells** and parts of cells called **platelets**.

White blood cells are made in the **bone marrow**. White cells gather together in the spleen, tonsils, adenoids, appendix and small intestine. They can also gather in the lymph nodes. The **lymph system** contains a liquid that transports white blood cells to the site of an **infection**. It then brings micro-organisms and dead cells back to the lymph nodes where they can be broken down and removed from the body.

> ## Question
>
> 2 Blood and lymph fluid travel all around the body. How might this help to protect us from infections and disease?

Your body's defences

micro-organisms are moved
along the surface of the cell

mucus-
producing
cell

Figure 2 Human Skin

Your skin helps to stop micro-organisms entering your body. If you breathe in any micro-organisms, hairs in your nose and tiny hairs on the surface of cells lining your trachea (windpipe) trap them.

Whenever a micro-organism enters the body, white blood cells race towards the site of infection. Different types of white blood cell attack infections in different ways. Some produce chemicals, called **antibodies**, which destroy the micro-organisms. White blood cells only live for a short time. A small drop of blood can contain between 7000 and 25 000 white blood cells. The more difficult an infection is to deal with, the more white blood cells are present in the blood.

Doctors can count the number of red and white blood cells in a small drop of blood and this can help the doctor decide how healthy you are.

> ## Question
>
> 3 Apart from special organs, what other ways has the body got to protect us from getting infected with a micro-organism?

> ## Remember
>
> Copy the following paragraph into your exercise book.
>
> The body has special glands and cells to help us fight infection. Infections can be spread in a number of ways (remember the five ways!). White blood cells help us fight off infection. Your nose acts as a filter trapping particles of dust and some micro-organisms, so you should breathe in through your nose and out through your mouth!

A shot in the arm

Key words

vaccination A way of protecting people against diseases

variolation An old way of protecting people from disease developed by the Chinese

Read the story of how a killer disease was stopped and in small groups discuss the questions at the bottom of the next page.

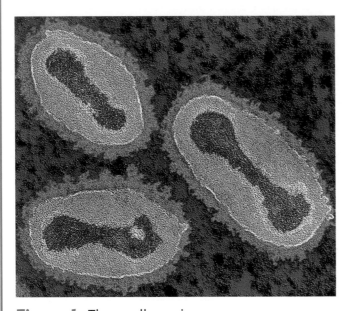

Figure 1 The smallpox virus

The disease smallpox has been known for over 2000 years. When people catch smallpox, sores show on the surface of their skin and in and around their mouth. These are called 'pocks'. They are produced by a virus. Smallpox was a deadly disease that killed millions of people, rich and poor.

Smallpox first appeared in China and the Far East. The Chinese developed a way of protecting people called **variolation**. They picked the scabs off infected people and dried them. They then ground the scabs into a fine dust. This dust was blown up the noses of healthy people. People protected in this way rarely caught smallpox. If they did, it was not as severe and did not always kill them.

The disease reached Europe around the year 710 and was taken to South America in the sixteenth century. Hernando Cortez, from Spain, invaded South America in 1520. The native Aztecs caught smallpox from the Spanish soldiers. Over 3 500 000 native South American people died from this disease in just 2 years. Smallpox has now been stamped out. The last outbreak was in Somalia in Africa on 26th October 1977.

Figure 2 Edward Jenner

Edward Jenner, a country doctor, is thought to have been the first person to discover **vaccination**. Jenner had noticed that milkmaids who caught cowpox seemed to be protected against smallpox. So in 1796 he deliberately infected a 9 year old boy, James Phipps, with cowpox by making a small scratch with a thorn on his arm. He took pus from a cowpox sore on the hand of a milkmaid called Sarah Nelmes and put it on the scratch on James' arm. Luckily James survived.

Figure 3 Lady Mary Wortley Montagu who protected her son from smallpox

Lady Mary Wortley Montagu saw children being protected against smallpox 78 years before Jenner made his discovery.

She was the wife of the British Ambassador to what is now Turkey. In 1715, she caught smallpox. She survived but her face was badly scarred by the sores and she lost her eyelashes!

In 1718 she had her 6 year old son protected from smallpox. Women in the villages in Turkey used walnut shells to collect the pus from sores of infected people. They would then dip a needle or sharp point into the pus and puncture the skin of the healthy children of the village. The children often got a little sick but soon recovered and were protected from smallpox.

Questions

Questions to think about and discuss:

1 Edward Jenner was a doctor who carried out an 'experiment' on James Phipps. Do you think he would be allowed to do the same today?

2 Was his 'experiment' a proper one to do?

3 What could have happened to the boy?

Remember

Write a short newspaper story telling how vaccination against smallpox was discovered.

AIDS

Key words

immune system   Protects your body from disease

vaccine   Liquid used to vaccinate people

symptoms   The effects of the disease on your body

What is AIDS?

AIDS is a disease that is caused by a virus called HIV. The HIV virus attacks the **immune system**. The immune system then doesn't work properly and cannot protect the people against other diseases and illnesses.

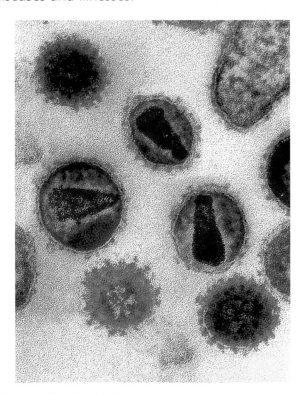

Figure 1   The AIDS virus

Where did HIV come from?

The first reported case of HIV was in 1981. It quickly spread and now many millions of people have the disease. Why did this disease suddenly appear in humans? Doctors are not sure where HIV came from. A similar disease is found in monkeys, but diseases don't usually jump from one species to another. Some scientists think that a **vaccine** made using tissue from monkeys allowed the virus to spread to humans.

Other scientists disagree. They say that people had come into contact with monkey blood before, so there was plenty of opportunity for humans to catch the disease from monkeys, but this never happened. Scientists need to do more experiments to find out where HIV came from.

Questions

1   What microorganism causes AIDS?

2   Describe how AIDS affects people.

How is the HIV virus spread?

HIV is normally spread in two ways. Having unprotected sex (sex without a condom) with someone who is HIV positive (they have the virus), or by having contact with blood from someone with HIV.

People who share needles when they inject themselves with drugs are also at risk. If one user is infected with HIV, then small amounts of their blood left in the needle can be injected into the healthy person. The virus can then infect the healthy person. There is also a very small risk that doctors and nurses could prick themselves accidentally with a syringe needle, so they have to take great care when using syringes.

HIV and AIDS cannot be caught easily. You won't catch the virus by sharing everyday items with someone who has HIV. You cannot get the virus by sharing or sitting on toilet seats or using the same swimming pool, bath or shower as an infected person. The virus is not spread by biting insects or through the air.

How does the HIV virus attack the body?

The virus gets into the white blood cells and takes them over. It tells the cell to make millions of copies of the virus. After a while the white blood cell bursts and releases the new viruses into the bloodstream and they infect other white blood cells. Eventually a person's immune system is destroyed and they can no longer fight off other infections.

Questions

3   How can drug users spread the HIV virus?

4   How do you think HIV destroys a person's immune system?

What are the symptoms of HIV?

When someone is infected with the HIV virus it can take a long time before any **symptoms** show. People who are infected with HIV may not develop AIDS for many years. Eventually when their immune system is almost destroyed, infected people will catch lots of different illnesses. Because they cannot fight them off, even a simple illness like a cold can be very serious. They often die from illnesses that most of us easily recover from, like pneumonia.

Question

5   How can a simple cold be dangerous to a person suffering from AIDS?

How are AIDS and HIV treated?

A lot of research has been put into developing a cure. The problem is that it is very difficult to stop any diseases caused by a virus. What the scientists have done is try to stop the HIV virus from copying itself in the white blood cells. A new drug called AZT helps. AZT slows down the copying process, but it cannot destroy the virus or stop it from being spread from one person to another. AZT slows the HIV virus down but it does not cure the disease.

How can we prevent HIV and AIDS from spreading?

The only way to stop the HIV virus from spreading is to make sure that people who are infected do not put other people at risk. This means that they should not have unprotected sex (sex without using a condom). People who use syringes and needles must never share needles. Doctors, nurses, dentists or ambulance drivers, must wear protective clothing and surgical gloves.

Questions

6   How does AZT help people infected with HIV?

7   What are the two main ways of preventing the spread of HIV and AIDS?

Finishing off!

Remember

Copy and complete the paragraph using the words in the list below:

**penicillin   brewing   yeast   bacteria   Alexander Fleming
Howard Florey   air-borne   insect-borne   fungi**

Germs can make us ill. Germs are usually divided into three groups, **b**_____,
viruses and **f**_____. Not all micro-organisms are harmful. Some like **y**_____
can be helpful and are used in baking and **b**_____. Others, like
p_____, are used to kill off bacteria. Penicillin was discovered by
A_____ **F**_____ and developed as a useful drug by
H_____ **F**_____ and Ernst Chain in the 1940s. Diseases can
be spread in a number of ways:

- Person-to-person
- Food-borne
- Water-borne
- A_____
- I_____.

Choose the correct word from the pairs given and copy the completed paragraph
into your exercise book.

The body has a number of cells and **organs/drugs** that are designed to help us
fight off infection. Our blood plays an important part in protecting us against
infection. Half of our blood is made up of **gas/cells** There are three types of cells
present in blood, **red/blue** cells that carry oxygen, white cells that fight off
tiredness/infection and platelets, bits of cells, that help blood to clot when we
have a cut.

Question

1   Take a new page in your exercise book. Make a list of all the Keywords from the
boxes in this chapter down the side. Take two lines per word. Try to write the
meaning of each word without looking. Then go back and fill in any you did not
know or got wrong. Now learn to spell them by the look–say–cover–write method.

Web sites to visit:

People and discoveries – Alexander Fleming
    http://www.pbs.org/wgbh/aso/databank/entries/bmflem.html

Smallpox story
    http://www.tulane.edu/~dmsander/Tutorials/Pox/Pox1.html

CHAPTER 8

Weathering and erosion

People are not sure what Stonehenge is. Some people think it's a temple. It took lots of people, lots of effort and lots of time to build it.

The huge granite stones have a mass of 25 tons each. We know they were carried there from Wales. But why?

The people who built Stonehenge wanted it to last. If they had used local stone, the weather would have made it crumble. The pillars would soon have fallen down. The building would just be a pile of stones in a field. So they used granite because it is a very hard rock.

Builders choose their natural materials carefully.

Stonehenge

The site of Stonehenge

1 Describe what these natural materials look and feel like.

   **clay   chalk   marble   sand   slate
   granite   sandstone**

2 Think of a use for each of the materials in Question 1. Choose uses in the building industry if possible.

3 Explain the difference between 'earth' and 'The Earth'.

4 What is the difference between 'sandy soil' and 'peaty soil'?

5 Why do farmers add fertiliser to the soil?

The scrubbed face of Britain

Key words

erosion   Rock gets broken up and carried away by wind and water

limestone   A hard rock that dissolves slowly in rain water

pot holes   Underground caves

weathering   Rock being broken up by the weather

The surface of the Earth is being changed by the weather.

Have you ever sanded a piece of wood? The rough surface gets turned into tiny dust particles as you rub. Then when you have finished, the surface is very smooth.

The surface of the Earth is being worn smooth by **weathering**. The wind and rain are wearing away the surface. Heating and freezing split the rocks up. Wind and water carry the bits away. This is called **erosion**.

Box 2

Figure 2 Edinburgh Castle

There have been volcanic eruptions and lava flows even in the United Kingdom.

Edinburgh Castle is built on a lump of hard granite rock formed by a volcano. This was left behind when the softer rock surrounding it was worn away.

Box 1

Figure 1 Limestone rocks

Under this moorland, the rock is full of caves.

Rainwater is a very weak acid, because it dissolves carbon dioxide from the air. Rain water falls on to the **limestone** and finds its way underground through tiny cracks. There it dissolves the rock away very slowly until huge caves are formed in the rock. People climb down and explore these 'pot holes'.

Box 3

Figure 3 Layers of rock at Lulworth Cove

The Earth's surface is not really 'rock solid' – it's moving about all the time. Sometimes these movements are quick jerks. These are earthquakes. Other rock movements are slow, steady pushes that take millions of years. These fold the rock layers into new shapes like the ones in the photo.

Box 4

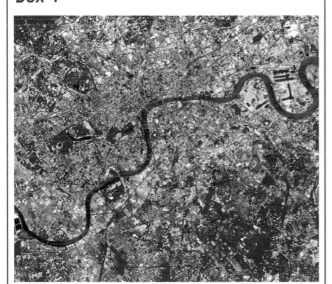

Figure 4 The River Thames

As The River Thames passes through London, its flow gets slower and slower and the river gets wider and wigglier. As the river slows down, all the tiny sand and mud particles it carries begin to settle out. These particles make the huge mud flats of the Thames Estuary.

Box 5

Figure 5 Danger! Rock falls

Why a danger notice? All these fallen stones were once high up on the mountainside.

As the rocks get heated by the Sun and then cool they expand and contract. When water in the rocks freezes it expands. These processes cause lumps of rock to crack and fall from the mountain. The danger sign tells people to be careful of falling rocks.

Questions

Box 1 How are potholes formed?

Box 2 Why has a lump of rock been left sticking up in Edinburgh?

Box 3 What caused the folding of the rock layers in Lulworth?

Box 4 Look at the picture in Box 4. Why do you think this shows a slow moving river rather than a fast river?

Box 5 What broke the rock from the mountain side?

Remember

Copy and complete the sentences. Use these words:

freezing   Earth   caves   water

The surface of the **E**_____ is being worn away by the wind and moving **w**_____.
Heating and **f**_____ breaks rocks up. Under the ground huge **c**_____ are formed when rock dissolves.

Rocks and minerals

Key words

grains Little bits

igneous rock This is made when molten rock becomes solid

metamorphic rock Made when other rock gets heated and squashed together

mineral A single solid substance

molten Melted

rock A mixture of different grains of minerals stuck together

sedimentary rock Made from particles carried by water and laid down in layers

Our planet is semi liquid inside. Only the outer 50 km has cooled to be solid **rock**. Millions of years of weather has made a lot of changes to this thin outer skin of our planet.

Rocks are mixtures of substances called **minerals**. Minerals are just one pure substance, and they are one colour.

Rocks are a mixture of colours. Rocks often look speckled. Erosion has mixed the **grains** of minerals together to make different rocks.

There are three groups of rock types. These are:

- **igneous rocks** – formed from **molten** material from the middle of the Earth;

- **sedimentary rocks** – formed when water deposits layers of material, one on top of another;

- **metamorphic rocks** – formed by the action of heat and pressure on other rocks.

Name of the mineral	What it looks like	What it's made of
quartz		silicon dioxide
olivine		magnesium iron silicate
feldspar		potassium aluminium silicate
malachite		copper carbonate
iron pyrites		iron sulphide
calcite		calcium carbonate
diamond		pure carbon
rock salt		sodium chloride

Table 1 Minerals

Rock type	Description	Type	Density	One source in UK
Conglomerates	A hard rock, like large pebbles held together. Looks a bit like concrete	Sedimentary	Medium	Devon
Sandstone	A crumbly rock made of sand-sized particles stuck together.	Sedimentary	Low	Just about anywhere!
Limestone	A hard rock made of calcium carbonate	Sedimentary	Medium	Portland
Chalk	A soft crumbly rock made from calcium carbonate shells of prehistoric sea animals	Sedimentary	Low	Dover
Mudstone	A soft rock made of tiny, tiny particles	Sedimentary	Medium	Just about anywhere!
Shale	A mudrock made from lots of thin layers	Sedimentary	Medium	Pembroke
Slate	Very hard black rock made of layers that can be made into flakes	Metamorphic	High	Pembroke
Marble	Very hard pretty rock	Metamorphic	High	Skye
Granite	A hard coarse grained rock	Igneous	Medium	Wales
Gabbro	A different coarse grained rock	Igneous	High	Lake District
Pumice	Soft and full of holes. Like a rock sponge	Igneous	Low	None
Obsidian	Dark glassy smooth rock	Igneous	High	Isle of Arran

Table 2 Rocks

Questions

1. What are the three main groups of rock types?

2. Draw what you would expect a conglomerate rock to look like.

3. Name two rocks that you would not use for building a wall?

4. What would the texture of these rocks be like?
   a) sandstone
   b) mudstone
   c) marble
   d) obsidian

Remember

Copy the table below. Put the materials in the list into the correct column.

**granite   diamond   quartz   slate
chalk   malachite   marble
iron pyrites**

These materials are rocks	These pure substances are minerals

A million year mixer 1

Key words

chemical weathering   Chemical reactions break up the rocks

mechanical weathering   Forces from wind, freezing, heating and rain break up the rocks

onion skin weathering   Layers peel off the rocks

Weathering

Wind and water break up rocks. This is called 'weathering'. There are two types of weathering: **mechanical weathering** and **chemical weathering**.

Part 1: Mechanical weathering

Freezing

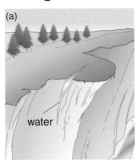

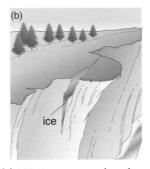

a) Water can fill cracks in the rock. If it is cold, the water will freeze.

b) Water expands when it freezes.

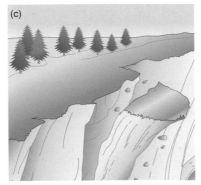

c) When this is repeated several times, it splits the rock.

Figure 1

Expansion

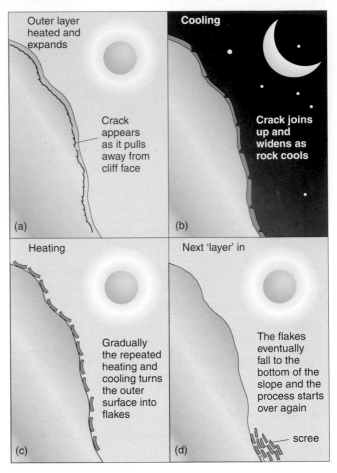

Figure 2 In the hot sun, one side of a rock can heat and expand while the other stays cool. The expansion of the heated rock can cause it to split.

The process in Figure 2 is called **onion skin weathering**. Layers peel off the rock a little at a time. The force of the expansion causes the layer to split off with a crack. This sometimes throws fragments of rock several metres.

Powerful plants

Seeds can grow in the cracks of rocks. The roots force themselves into the cracks, making them bigger. Next time you walk down a tree-lined street, look at the roots of the trees. They often crack paving stones and force pavements up as they grow. They can do the same to rocks. All of this is part of mechanical weathering.

Wind

Figure 3

The odd shapes of the rock in Figure 3 are caused by strong winds blowing sand over them. This wears away softer rock from under harder rock.

Sea

Figure 4

Waves smash into the coast. This breaks off parts of the cliffs. The waves roll the rocks back and forth, making them into smaller and smaller pieces.

Glacier

Figure 5 This valley in Switzerland was shaped by the movement of a glacier.

Huge heavy sheets of ice break up rock and carry it away. The landscape produced has steep sided 'U' shaped valleys rather than 'V' shaped river valleys.

Questions

1 When water freezes it expands. If water pipes freeze there can be a problem. Explain why?

2 What is 'onion skin weathering'?

3 Only hard stone like granite is used for gravestones. Why is this?

4 Make three drawings to show the effect of plant roots. Picture A should show soil in a crack in a rock. Picture B has a seed germinating in it. Picture C has the big plant roots forcing the crack wider.

Remember

Copy and complete the sentences. Use these words:

carry   freezes   crack   water   peel

Mechanical weathering happens when:

● water **f**_____ in cracks in the rock and splits the rock.

● heat expands one side of a rock and not the other, making it **p**_____ away.

● plant roots can force apart a **c**_____ in a rock.

● Running **w**_____ or wind **c**_____ the pieces of rock away.

A million year mixer 2

Figure 1 Limestone caves in Barbados.

Part 2: Chemical weathering

Chemicals in the air and water can change rocks. Rainwater is naturally slightly acid. Carbon dioxide dissolves in rainwater to make a weak acid called **carbonic acid**.

Limestone caves

Limestone is alkaline, so it reacts with the acid in rain water. Limestone contains calcium carbonate. This dissolves in rain water to make calcium hydrogen carbonate solution.

calcium carbonate (solid)	+	carbonic acid (rainwater)	→	calcium hydrogen carbonate (solution)

As rain water trickles through cracks in the limestone over many years, it can dissolve millions of tonnes of rock to make huge caves.

The dissolved rock in the underground water is not very stable. It will slowly turn into rock again. A steady drip from the ceiling will form the **stalactites** like in the photo.

Hard water

Water from chalky areas has calcium compounds dissolved in it. It is given the name **hard water**. Hard water is very healthy to drink, as we need calcium and other minerals in our bodies.

But hard water does cause problems. It forms scum with soap and leaves the **lime scale** that is found in kettles. Water softeners can remove the dissolved calcium compounds.

Questions

1 Why is rain slightly acid?

2 Why is limestone attacked more than other types of rock?

3 Why is hard water healthy to drink?

Acid rain pollution

Figure 2 A statue damaged by acid rain

Some rain water is polluted. It has acid substances in it caused by burning fossil fuels. This stronger **acid rain** badly damages buildings and monuments, particularly those made out of limestone or marble.

But it's not just limestone and marble that get attacked. Many hard rocks such as granite contain alkaline minerals. The acid rainwater will dissolve minerals out of the hard rocks. This makes the rock softer, so erosion is easier.

Questions

4 Put the garden statues in date order, starting with the oldest one. The dates are: 1789, 1852, 1906, 1979.

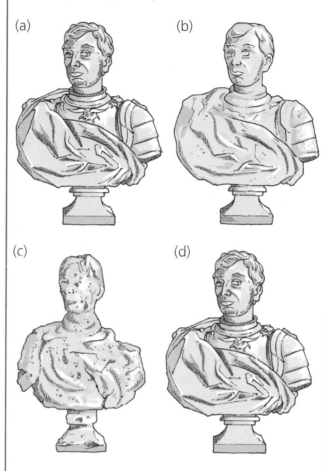

(a)　　(b)

(c)　　(d)

5 Rainwater is normally only slightly acid. How can pollution make it more acid?

Remember

Copy and complete the sentences. Use these words:

dissolve　acid　weathering

Chemical **w**_____ happens when water or dilute acids slowly **d**_____ rock. **A**____ rain speeds up the process.

Canyon story

Key words

boulders   Very big rocks

estuary   River mouth where the river meets the sea

flash floods   Floods that form very quickly

Grand Canyon   Very big valley in America

gravel   Small stones up to a few centimetres in size

sediment   Solid rocky material laid down by a river

shallow   Not deep

upstream   Away from the river mouth

The soil in the Grand Canyon is baked by the Sun and is very hard. It cannot absorb water when the rains come. The plants that grow in the Grand Canyon have very **shallow** root systems.

When there is a lot of rain, there are no deep plant roots holding the soil and rock in place. Often **flash floods** can move **boulders** the size of cars, buses and even small houses.

The Colorado River has spring floods of 10 000 tonnes of water per second. This means that if you were standing near the river, 10 000 tonnes of water would flow past you every second! All of the melting snow in the Rocky Mountains comes pouring down through the Grand Canyon in May and June every year, as regular as clock-work.

The Colorado River's spring floods used to carry away all of the rocks that were in the main channel. This has worn away the bed of the river with all of this fast-moving material.

Over the last 20 million years the Colorado River has dug a very famous trench. It is 30 km wide, 450 km long and 1.5 km (a mile) deep! The **Grand Canyon** was formed by water (and ice) and by wind. But water has done most of the work.

Figure 1 The Grand Canyon in Arizona, USA.

The banks of the river have been slowly eaten away. The river has widened and cut down deeper into the lower rock layers, making the one mile deep trench it flows through today.

Questions

1 Where is the Grand Canyon?

2 Why does the soil get washed away so easily in this area?

3 Why is spring the worst season for erosion in the Colorado River?

4 How big are the rocks that get carried along by the flash floods?

Gravel and mud flats

The River Thames has a shallow, wide valley, not like the deep trench of the Grand Canyon. All along the river valley material has been carried by the running water. This material has been sorted by size, according to how fast the river was flowing. It is laid down as a **sediment**.

Upstream from London there are deposits of **gravel**. These settled out as the river slowed on its way to the sea. This gravel has been dug out leaving big holes which fill with water.

Smaller sandy particles are lighter than gravel, so they got carried further. They settled out in what is now the London area. The ground is very sandy there. Tiny particles got carried furthest, but even these settled out when the river widened at the sea. They have made the mud flats of the Thames **Estuary**.

Weathering mixes up the minerals in rock, then flowing water carries them away and sorts them out by size.

Questions

5 Why are there gravel deposits to the west of London?

6 Why are sandy beaches found near river mouths?

Remember

Draw a cross-section along a river bed. Draw it from mountains to the sea. Show these sections:

- Fast flowing – picks up material
- Fast flowing – material gets broken up
- Medium flow – large particles settle out
- Slow flow – small particles settle out
- Stopped at the seas – mud settles out

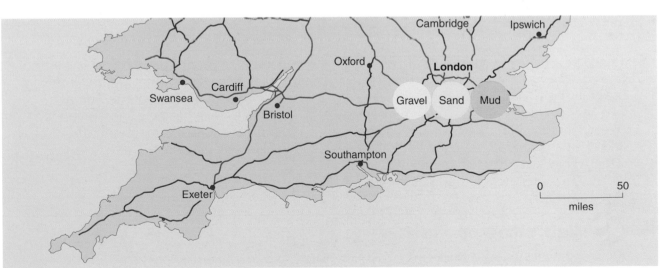

Figure 2 The London Basin

Finishing off!

Changing landscape, changing life

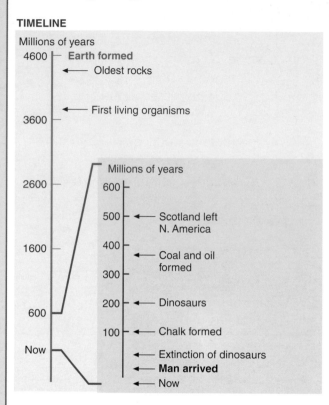

TIMELINE

Millions of years

4600 — Earth formed
← Oldest rocks

3600 — ← First living organisms

Millions of years

2600 — 600 —

500 — ← Scotland left N. America

1600 — 400 —
← Coal and oil formed
300 —

200 — ← Dinosaurs

600 — 100 — ← Chalk formed

Now — ← Extinction of dinosaurs
← **Man arrived**
← Now

There are two processes which shape the surface of the Earth.

1 The Earth's surface is divided into big slabs, bigger than continents, called **tectonic plates**. These move about, pushing up mountains, making earthquakes and volcanoes.

2 Erosion smooths out the surface, levels the mountains and flattens the volcanoes.

Sometimes outside events have an influence on the surface of the Earth. Sixty-three million years ago a terrible event shattered life for the dinosaurs. Scientists think that a big meteorite collided with the Earth. The meteorite was only 10 kilometres in diameter, but it had a huge effect.

Dust was thrown into the air. This dust took years to settle. During this time it blocked the Sun's rays from the Earth. The Earth's surface cooled so much that the dinosaurs struggled to survive. In quite a short period the dinosaurs, who had ruled the Earth for 180 million years, died out. We know this because erosion has uncovered their fossil remains.

Sixty million years after the dinosaurs became extinct the first man-like creatures appeared.

Questions

1 Take a new page in your exercise book. Make a list of all the Key Words from the boxes in this chapter down the side. Take two lines per word. Try to write the meaning of each word without looking. Then go back and fill in any you did not know or got wrong. Now learn to spell them by the look–say–cover–write method.

2 Choose one event from the time line in the picture above. Draw what you think the event would have looked like. Add a newspaper style headline and caption to your picture. Use a computer for the headline and captions.

Web sites to visit:

Essential Guide to Rocks
http://www.bbc.co.uk/education/rocks/index.shtml

Science Across the World: Acid Rain
http://www.scienceacross.org/english/the_topics/index/html

Light

Starter Activity
Seeing the light

We can see because light travels from light sources like the Sun or light bulbs and enters our eyes. Our eyes detect light. We see things when the light from these light sources enters our eyes.

Opaque objects do not let light travel through them. They create shadows on a sunny day.

We can see clearly through some materials like glass and water. They let light travel through them. These materials are **transparent**.

Hold a thin plastic cup to a strong light and it will let light come through, but you won't be able to see through it. Materials which let light through, but which you can't see through are **translucent**.

The woman is **opaque** and casts a shadow on the ground. The clouds are **translucent**, light passes through but we can't see through them. The woman's glasses are **transparent**, she can see through them.

Questions

1 What do you call your light detectors?

2 What must light do so that you can see something?

3 List three things that are:

a) transparent

b) translucent

c) opaque.

Sources of light

The Sun is a source of light, and so are light bulbs, candles and camera flashguns. Light spreads out from sources.

Light shines into a camera through the lens at the front. It shines onto the film. The film changes. Where the light is brightest, the film changes the most. The pattern on the film matches the light that shines onto it. We call the pattern a photograph.

Figure 3   The flashgun gives a quick burst of light. Movie stars have to get used to bright lights.

Figure 1   The candle is a weak source of light. The light does not have much effect on the film inside the camera.

Figure 2   The Sun is a really strong source of light. It provides enough light for a good photograph.

Figure 4   The Sun is our natural source of light. When the Sun sets it goes dark. After sunset we have to use artificial lighting if we want to see anything.

Inside your eye

Inside a camera

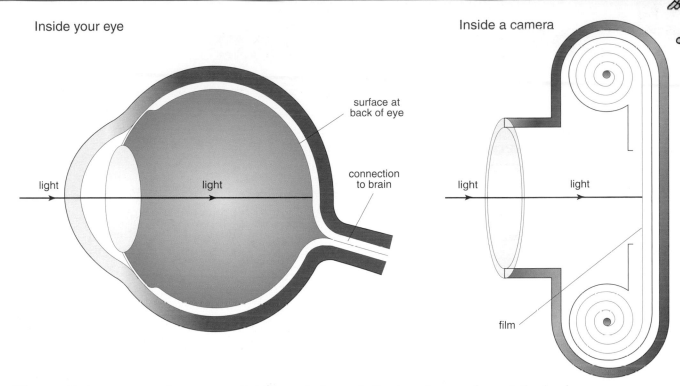

surface at
back of eye

connection
to brain

light

light

light

light

film

Figure 5 In an eye and a camera, light travels through the lens to a surface at the back.

Your eye is a bit like a camera. The front of your eye is transparent so light can shine in. The light passes through the eye **lens** onto a surface at the back. The light produces changes in the surface. The changes are passed through nerves connected to your brain, and that's how you see.

The speed of light

Light travels very fast indeed. Its speed is 300 000 kilometres per second! Light takes just over 8 minutes to travel from the Sun to Earth, a distance of 150 million kilometres (93 million miles).

In the time it takes to blink your eye, light could travel from Manchester to London one hundred times. The speed of sound is much slower. It only travels 330 metres in one second. That's almost a million times slower.

Questions

1   Is the room that you are in lit by sunlight or by artificial light or both?

2   Make a list of different kinds of artificial light.

Remember

Copy and complete the sentences. Use these words:

**film   Sun   transparent   speed
sources of light   photograph**

Light must enter our eyes so that we can see. The light comes from **s___ o_ l___** such as the **S__** and camera flashes. It travels at very high **s___**. Light can shine through **t___** materials such as the fronts of our eyes or the lens in front of a camera. The light that reaches the **f__** in a camera makes a **p___**. The light that reaches the back of our eyes lets us see.

Reflections and straight lines

Key words

reflection The return of light from a surface

texture Whether a surface is rough or smooth

We know that mirrors reflect light. You can also see your '**reflection**' when you look into a still pool of water. Mirrors and water have very smooth surfaces. They give us very clear reflections.

Figure 1 shows a cave painting in Lascaux in France. It was painted 17 000 years ago. It shows the animals people hunted. For thousands of years the painting was in darkness. Then about a hundred years ago people went into the caves with lamps. The light spread out from their lamps. It reached the surfaces all around. The surfaces reflected the light. Some of the light reached the eyes of the people.

Figure 1 Cave painting from Lascaux in France. The surface of the rock has different textures – there are rough areas and smoother areas.

Different surfaces reflect light in different ways. There are shiny pools of water on the floor. The water surfaces are smooth like mirrors. There are the rough surfaces of the rock. The **texture** of a surface affects how it looks to us.

The light from most sources is white or nearly white. White surfaces reflect a lot of light. Black surfaces reflect very little light. Coloured surfaces only reflect some kinds of light.

Light travels in straight lines

Light from a source spreads out and travels in straight lines. We can test this by looking down a piece of rubber tubing. We can see through it only when it is in a straight line. You may have seen the ray of light from a laser.

Figure 2 A ray is the pathway of a very narrow beam of light. It is much easier to think about how light is reflected if we just think about a single ray.

Questions

1 a) Where is the light coming from for you to see this book?

b) What does the surface of the book do to the light?

2 Mirrors are very good reflectors of light. What is special about the surfaces of mirrors?

3 Which is better at reflecting light, a white surface or a black surface?

4 Why can't you see round corners?

Remember

Copy and complete the sentences. Use these words:

**white   reflect   lines   texture
sources   colour**

We see surfaces because light from **s___** spreads out and the surfaces **r___** it. The **t___** of a surface makes a difference to how it looks to us. We can't see clear reflections from rough surfaces. Surfaces also affect the **c___** of the light that reaches our eyes. Light from most light sources is **w___** or nearly white. Light travels in straight **l___**.

Seeing ourselves

Key words

angle of incidence The angle between the normal and the ray of light striking the surface

angle of reflection The angle between the normal and the ray of light reflected from the surface

invert To turn upside down or back to front

normal A line drawn at 90° to a surface

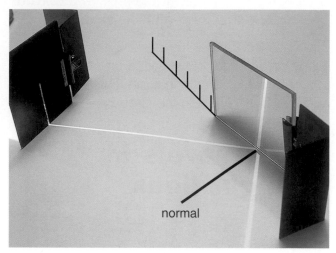

Figure 2 In the experiment, the ray box and mirror are set up like this. Next the position of the two rays will be marked on with a pencil.

Mirrors

The picture you see of your face in a mirror is called an image of your face.

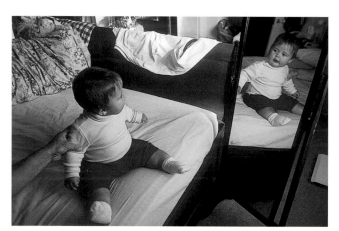

Figure 1 This baby is looking at its image in a mirror.

In Figure 1, light from all parts of the baby's face is reflected to its eyes. The baby sees an image which is behind the mirror, the same size and the right way up.

If you hold some writing in front of a mirror you will find that it is back to front. We say it **inverts** back to front.

We can make measurements on a ray of light when it falls onto a mirror.

First we mark the position of the mirror, then we draw a **normal** line. It is an imaginary line that sticks straight out at 90° to the mirror. We draw it at the point where the ray of light is reflected.

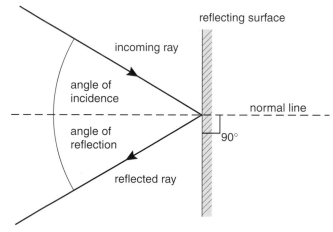

Figure 3 The reflection of a single ray by a mirror.

Then we can measure the angles the ray makes before and after it is reflected. These are **angle of incidence** and the **angle of reflection**. We can change the angle of incidence and measure the angle of reflection each time.

The results of an experiment have been recorded in Table 1. What is the relationship between the two?

Angle of incidence	Angle of reflection
14°	14°
26°	25°
38°	39°

Table 1 Some results from an experiment to measure the angle of incidence and angle of reflection from a mirror.

The angle of incidence and angle of reflection are variables. We control the size of the angle of incidence, so we call it the input variable. As a result we measure the angle of reflection so we call it the output variable.

There is a simple relationship between these two variables. The angle of incidence and angle of reflection are always the same. This discovery is called the law of reflection.

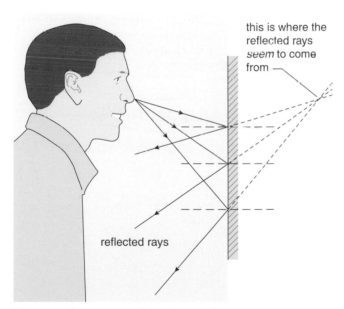

this is where the reflected rays *seem* to come from

reflected rays

Figure 4 We can draw just a few rays spreading from a point on a face. The rays all obey the law of reflection. The rays seem to be coming from a point somewhere inside the mirror – that's where we see the image.

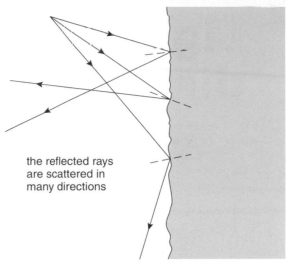

the reflected rays are scattered in many directions

Figure 5 Mirrors have very smooth surfaces. Rough surfaces can also reflect light, but they don't produce clear images. The bumps on the surface reflect light in different directions. Reflection like this is called scattering of the light.

Questions

1 Which of these are correct drawings of reflection and which are wrong?

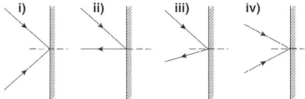

2 a) What is the name of the law that rays obey when they are reflected?
   b) Write down this law.

Remember

Copy and complete the sentences. Use these words:

**output   ray   variable   images
angle   scatter   law   reflection**

When a **r__** of light is reflected by a mirror, the **a___** of incidence is always equal to the angle of **r___**. This is called the **l__** of reflection. In an experiment on reflection, the angle of incidence is the input **v___** and the angle of reflection is the **o___** variable. Rough surfaces do not produce clear **i___** but **s___** the light.

Light changing direction

Key words

refraction   The change in path of light as it passes between different materials

Figure 1   The pencil appears to bend at the water/air surface.

Light can change direction when it passes from one transparent material to another. This bending of light is called **refraction**. Refraction happens at surfaces (such as water and glass surfaces) and can change the direction of the light.

Figure 2   Refraction of light through a glass block.

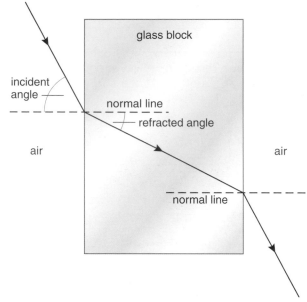

Figure 3   Glass surfaces refract light. To see just how much a ray is bent we can draw a normal line. We then measure the incident angle and the refracted angle. Notice that whether the light is going into the glass or coming out, the angle in the air is always the bigger one.

Question

1   Which diagrams show refraction correctly?

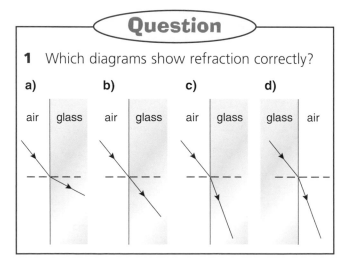

Light can play tricks

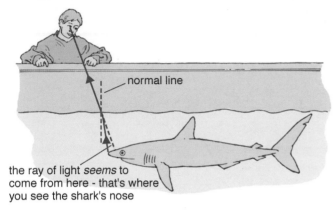

the ray of light *seems* to come from here - that's where you see the shark's nose

Figure 4 The shark is nearer than we think.

The nearest most of us ever get to a shark is at a 'deep sea centre'. When we look down into the shark tank we know that the shark will not be where it appears to be. Refraction has caused the rays of light from it to bend.

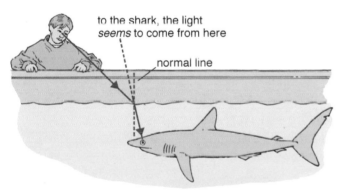

to the shark, the light *seems* to come from here

normal line

Figure 5 Refraction of light from the person confuses the shark.

It would need a clever shark to jump out and bite us. It would have to be good at jumping and know about refraction. When the shark looks up at you it can see you, but not in the right place.

The reappearing coin

Try this trick on your friends at home. Put a coin at the bottom of an empty cup. Ask them to move back until they just cannot see the coin. Challenge them to make it reappear without moving their head. Answer: pour some water in the cup and it will reappear.

2 a) Which position, x or y, shows where the person sees the shark's nose?

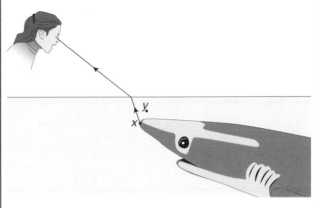

b) Write a sentence or two to explain why you think this.

Remember

Copy and complete the sentences. Use these words:

**incidence   rays   bigger   normal
refraction**

When light passes through a surface then **re_____** takes place. The pathway of the light can be bent. To someone watching from the side, the place where the **r___** of light seem to come from is not where they actually come from. To compare the sizes of the angle of **i___** and the angle of refraction we draw a **n___** line through the surface. Whichever way the light is travelling, the angle of incidence in the air is always **b___** than the angle in water or glass.

Colour movies

Figure 2 With colour film, different colours of light reach different parts of the screen.

The old films are in black and white. Each frame produces shadows on the screen. Black areas of the frame absorb the light and make dark shadows. Transparent areas of the frame let the light from the projector shine through. Then we see the bright light that's scattered off the screen. Grey areas of the frame absorb some of the light and let the rest shine through to the screen.

Now when we go to the cinema we usually see colour on the screen. Each frame has areas of colour to absorb some of the light from the projector. A red area of the frame lets only red light through. The screen reflects the red light to our eyes. A blue area of the film only lets blue light shine through. On the screen we see blue. The red and blue areas of the frame are acting as **filters**. They absorb some kinds of light but let other kinds travel through.

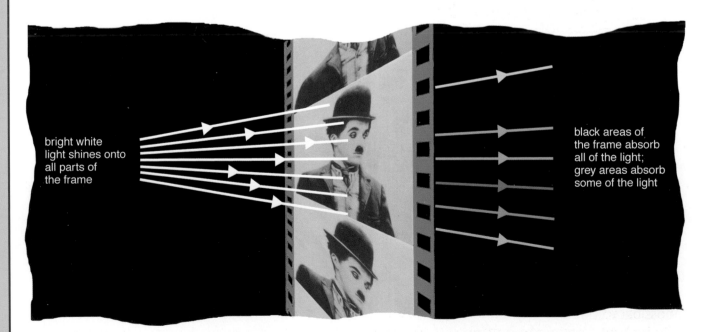

bright white light shines onto all parts of the frame

black areas of the frame absorb all of the light; grey areas absorb some of the light

Figure 1 Some areas of a film absorb part of the light and make shadows in shades of grey on the screen.

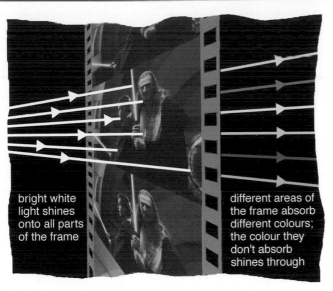

bright white light shines onto all parts of the frame

different areas of the frame absorb different colours; the colour they don't absorb shines through

Figure 3 Coloured areas of film act as filters – absorbing some colours of the light but letting others shine through to the screen.

The spectrum

Figure 4 Dispersion by a prism shows that white light is a mixture of all the colours.

From the white light of the projector it is possible to create any colour on the screen. White light seems to be a mixture of all colours.

We can try out this idea by shining a thin beam of light through a **prism**. What we see is a rainbow of colour called a **spectrum**. We can see that the prism has separated the light into its different colours. We say the prism has **dispersed** the light.

An object looks coloured because it only reflects certain colours of light. For example a blue flower will only reflect blue light. If white light falls on the flower, the red and green are absorbed. Blue light gets reflected to your eye, so the flower appears blue. In the same way, grass looks green because it absorbs red and blue light, and reflects green coloured light.

Questions

1 White light from a projector shines onto a frame of film. Describe the light that shines through areas of film that are:
   a) solid black
   b) grey
   c) red
   d) green.

2 A prism separates white light into colours.
   a) What is this process called?
   b) What kind of light would you see if you could mix the two colours up again?

Remember

Copy and complete the sentences. Use these words:

**green   spectrum   filters   absorb
white   pass   disperse**

Different areas of film **a**___ some colours but let others pass through. They act as colour **f**___. A green area of film, for example, lets green light **p**___ through. Then the screen scatters **g**___ light to our eyes.

A prism can **d**___ white light into a **s**___ of colours. This shows that **w**____ light is a mixture of coloured light.

Finishing off!

★ Light must enter our eyes so that we can see. Light can travel through space and through the air. It travels at high speed, much faster than the speed of sound.

★ Light travels from sources and falls onto surfaces. We see surfaces because they **reflect** or scatter the light.

★ When objects block the pathway of bright light, shadows are formed. In diagrams, the straight pathways of light are called rays.

★ A mirror has a very smooth surface. When a mirror reflects a ray of light the **angle of incidence** is always equal to the **angle of reflection**. Rough surfaces do not normally produce clear images.

★ When light passes from one substance to

another it can change direction. We say that **refraction** happens at the surface between the substances. We can draw rays to help us to think about refraction as well as reflection.

★ A **prism** can disperse white light into a **spectrum** of colours. This shows that white light is a mixture of coloured light. Some surfaces only reflect some of the colours.

★ Coloured areas of film absorb some colours but let other colours pass through. They act as colour **filters**.

★ Some objects appear coloured. They reflect certain colours of white light and absorb the other colours. The light reflected to the eye is the colour you see.

1 Take a new page in your exercise book. Make a list of all the Key Words from the boxes in this chapter down the side. Take two lines per word. Try to write the meaning of each word without looking. Then go back and fill in any you did not know or got wrong.

Now learn to spell them by the look–say–cover–write method.

2 Make careful sketches to show a ray of light
 a) being reflected by a mirror
 b) being refracted as it goes from air to glass.

3 Why can't you see your reflection in a rough surface?

4 Light gets refracted as it passes between air and water. Explain what refraction is.

5 Coloured objects often look strange when you see them under a coloured light. What colour would these snooker balls seem to be?
 a) a red ball in red light
 b) a red ball in blue light
 c) a blue ball in red light
 d) a green ball in white light
 e) a white ball in green light

Web sites to visit:

Making a simple camera
    http://www.exploratorium.edu/science_explorer/pringles_pinhole.html

Reflection and refraction
    http://library.thinkquest.org/10796/ch10/ch10.htm

CHAPTER 10

Ecological relationships

How many people are there in this photo? Don't try to count them, just have a guess. Human beings make up what we call a **population**. There are also lots of other types of plants and animals on the Earth. These also make up populations. This chapter will look at how these populations interact with each other and how living things within a community influence each other and can be affected by the environment.

Questions

1 Last year you did a unit of work on ecology. Can you remember the work you did on food chains and webs? Copy the words below into your exercise book and see if you can write a sentence about each one to explain what it means.

   ★ Food chain
   ★ Habitat
   ★ Producer
   ★ Food web

2 Here is a simple food web. Describe in a sentence what would take place if the following things happened:

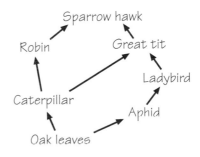

a) What would happen to the ladybirds if most of the aphids died?
b) What would happen to the numbers of caterpillars if the sparrowhawks ate lots of robins and great tits?
c) What would happen if the oak tree was cut back and lost lots of branches with leaves?

How many people are there in the world today?

How many people are there in your class? How many people are there in your school? Now try to imagine how many people there are in the world. It's very difficult. Imagine how difficult it is to know exactly how many people there actually are in the world.

The United States Government estimates how many people are living on the Earth at any one time. They guessed that the 6 **billionth** baby would be born on 19 July 1999 at about 12:24 in the morning. This means that there are over 6 million, million people alive today. Another organisation, the United Nations, said that the 6 billionth baby was a baby boy who was born in the Bosnian capital, Sarajevo, at 2 minutes past midnight local time on Tuesday 12 October 1999. The UN chose this as 'D6B', the Day of the 6 Billionth person.

The graph in Figure 2 shows how the world population has grown and how we think it will continue to grow into the new millennium.

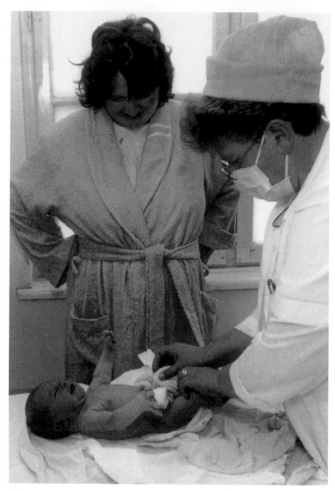

Figure 1 The 6 billionth person.

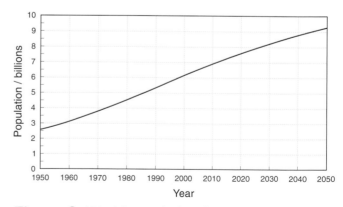

Figure 2 World population figures from 1950 to 2050 (Source: US Bureau of the Census)

Questions

1 About how many people were there in the world in 1950?

2 By how much has the world population grown since 1950?

3 How many people do we think there will be in the year 2025?

If the world **population** keeps on growing as fast as it is growing today, there will be lots of problems. Some countries find it difficult to grow enough food to feed their population. In other countries the amount of land that can be built on or used for housing is running out.

City	Population
London (UK)	6 967 500
Birmingham (UK)	1 008 400
Madrid (Spain)	3 041 101
Paris (France)	2 175 200
Bombay (India)	9 925 891
Mexico City (Mexico)	9 815 795
Beijing (China)	8 200 000
New York (USA)	7 333 253
Lahore (Pakistan)	5 085 000
Athens (Greece)	824 000

Table 1 The population of some big cities

Questions

4 Look at Table 1, it shows the population of some major cities. Make a table in your exercise book and put the cities in order from the biggest to the smallest. Use the headings from Table 1.

5 Which city has fewer than 1 million people?

6 Which city has nearly 5 times more people than Birmingham?

7 Which two cities have nearly 10 million people?

Remember

Match the first half of the sentence in column 1 to its correct tail in column 2 then copy the full sentence into your exercise book

The biggest city in the UK . . .	is Birmingham with over 1 million people.
The word billion means . . .	was born in the year 1999.
The second biggest city in the UK . . .	is London with nearly 7 million people.
The six billionth baby in the world . . .	a population.
All of the human beings in the world make . . .	of plants or animals of the same kind.
A population is any group . . .	a million million.

Predator vs prey

Key words

camouflage   A coat or skin colour that blends into the background making it hard to see an animal

predator   An animal that hunts, catches and eats other animals for food

prey   Animals that are hunted by predators for food

A **predator** is an animal that hunts, catches and eats other animals for food. The animals being hunted are called **prey**. Predators help to keep the numbers of prey down in an area. How many prey there are in an area will limit the numbers of predators that can live there.

Predators kill only the weakest prey. Animals are not necessarily always predators or always prey. For example, a stickleback fish may hunt and eat tadpoles. The stickleback may be hunted itself and eaten by a bigger fish called a roach.

Imagine you are a rabbit and you have just noticed a fox preparing to attack you. What would you do? You'd run! The fastest escape and survive. The slowest get caught.

Sometimes animals have features that look like enormous eyes so that they look bigger. Other animals can actually make themselves bigger.

Questions

1   What has the animal in Figure 1 done to try and prevent it from being eaten?

2   What else would make this animal difficult to eat?

Figure 1   The puffer fish inflates its body to make it difficult to eat and to make it look larger than it really is.

Figure 2 The hedgehog's spines make it a difficult meal to eat.

Pretending to be an animal that is dangerous to a predator is also a way of avoiding being eaten. Some animals have protection such as shells or spines. Hedgehogs are very difficult to eat because of their sharp spines.

Figure 3 The colour of the frog and its markings warn any predators that it should not be eaten.

Some animals make chemicals or poisons that can kill a predator or make them very sick. The poison arrow frog has a chemical on its skin that does this. Any animals that eat these small frogs are likely to get very sick or die. Poisonous animals are often brightly coloured to warn predators that they are not nice to eat.

Questions

3 A hedgehog does not have spines underneath its body. How does it protect its stomach if it is attacked?

4 Why do you think the frog in the picture is bright blue? What message might it be giving to any predators?

Figure 4 Where is the soldier in this photo?

Some animals hide themselves against the backgound. The colour and the patterns on their skins or coats hides them from potential danger. This is called **camouflage**. Soldiers use camouflage clothing to hide from their enemy. Can you see the soldier in Figure 4?

Questions

5 How does a stick insect try to prevent itself from being eaten?

6 Why does an elephant not need colours or stripes to blend into the background in the wild?

Predators have also developed features that help them to catch their prey. Predators with the best eyesight or hearing or those that can run fastest will catch more prey.

Remember

Write a sentence about how each of the following animals tries to stop itself being caught and eaten by a predator:

**puffer fish   hedgehog   hare
stick insect**

Now write a sentence about the features each of the following animals have that help them to catch their prey:

eagle   tiger   fox   house spider

Feeding habits

Key words

meadow   Open grassy field
vole   Small animal, like a mouse

The barn owl is a predator. Owls used to be a common sight in Great Britain. They live inside buildings (for example barns on farms), or inside large holes in trees and rock faces. Figure 1 shows where barn owls can be found in this country.

☐ – no barn owls in these areas

▧ – areas where barn owls are found

Figure 1   Barn owls can be found all over Britain.

Feeding habits

Barn owls eat lots of **voles** which are small mouse-like animals. Barn owls hunt in long grassy **meadows** where the voles live. Barn owls begin to breed in late February. The female will lay between 4–6 eggs in late April or May. About 30 days later the eggs will hatch. The young are fed and looked after by the parents for the next 2–3 months.

Figure 3 A barn owl with a mouse.

Key:
— Voles
— Owls

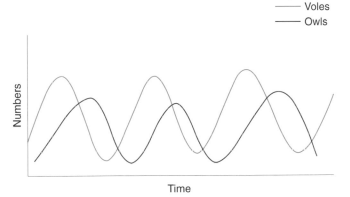

Time

Figure 2 Graph showing the feeding relationship between the barn owl and the vole.

Figure 2 shows you what might happen to the numbers of owls and voles as the owls hunt the voles in order to feed their mate and their chicks. When there are lots of voles, the number of owls goes up. This is because there are more voles for the owls to feed on, so more of their chicks survive. With less food the number of owls goes down because some of the chicks will starve and die. Can you see how the pattern for the number of owls follows the pattern for the number of voles?

Questions

1 Copy the graph in Figure 2 into your exercise book.

2 Barn owls aren't found in the highlands of Scotland where there aren't many meadows and grasslands. What might stop the barn owls nesting and living there?

3 Barn owls hunt at night. What does a barn owl have that makes it good at hunting at night?

4 Barn owl chicks need to be looked after for between 2 and 3 months. What do you think will happen to the number of voles during this time?

Remember

Choose the correct word from each pair and copy the completed paragraph into your exercise book. Think carefully before you choose!

Barn owls eat mostly voles. When there are **plenty of/fewer** voles, the owls produce **less/more** chicks. The number of owls goes **down/up**. This means that there are more **owls/voles** catching and eating the **owls/voles**. The number of voles goes **up/down**. With fewer voles there is **more/less** food for the owls and more owls die of starvation.

Looking at pyramids

Key words

biomass   How much of a living thing there is

pyramid of numbers   A way of showing the numbers of plants and animals in a food chain

pyramid of biomass   A way of showing how much the individuals in a food chain weigh

Look at the food chain in Figure 1. It is a simple food chain that you can find in a pond. The food chain tells you who eats what. Remember that food is a fuel that we use to release energy for living. The arrows show that the fuel is transferred from the pondweed to the tadpoles up to the heron as each one is eaten.

What the food chain doesn't show you is the number of plants and animals in the pond. We can show this with a **pyramid of numbers** like the one in Figure 2. One or two pondweed plants can feed lots of tadpoles. A few minnows will eat many tadpoles. Two perch can eat four or five minnows. One heron can eat a couple of perch.

The pyramid of numbers is useful but doesn't tell us about the amount of fuel and energy available to each link in the food chain. To find this out, we have to weigh the amount of plants and animals in each link of the chain. Then we can make a **pyramid of biomass** like the one in Figure 3.

Making a pyramid of biomass

Imagine taking all of the pondweed out of a pond and weighing it. If we did this we would find its mass (remember in science when we weigh things we find its mass!). Because it is a living thing and biology is the study of living things we call it a **biomass**. We can do the same for the tadpoles, the minnows, the perch and the herons. If we did this, then we would get a pyramid that looks like the one in Figure 3. As we move up the pyramid, the biomass gets a little smaller. So a pyramid of biomass tells us about the amount of fuel and energy that is available for each link in a food chain, the higher we go the less fuel there is and so less energy is released.

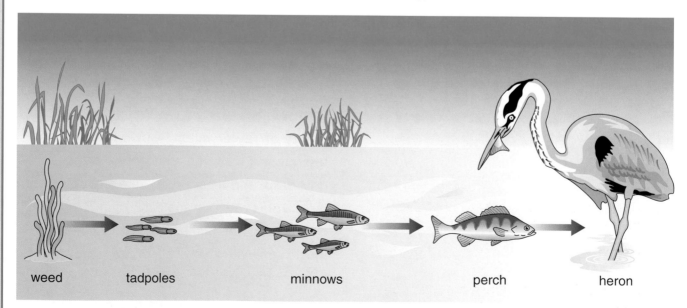

weed   tadpoles   minnows   perch   heron

Figure 1   A simple food chain.

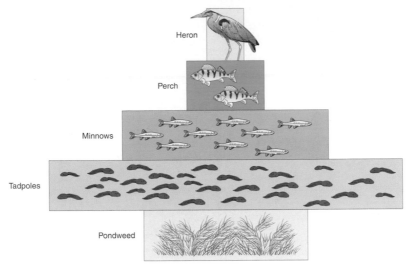

Figure 2 A pyramid of numbers.

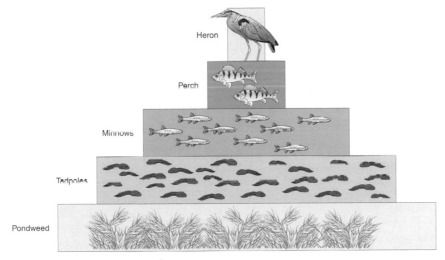

Figure 3 A pyramid of biomass.

Remember

Match the following terms with their definition.

Pyramid of numbers: shows how energy is transferred from one living thing to another.

Food chain: shows how many individuals there are in a food chain or a food web.

Food web: shows us how much the individuals in a food chain or web would weigh.

Pyramid of biomass: is made up of many food chains and shows us who eats what.

Questions

1   Draw a pyramid of numbers for the following food chain?

rosebush (1) → aphids (200) → ladybirds (5) → blackbird (2) → cat (1)

2   How can a single rosebush provide enough food for so many aphids?

The killing chain

It isn't just energy that is transferred in food chains. Chemicals sprayed on plants or put into streams and rivers can also move up food chains. Forty years ago a chemical called **DDT** was made as a pesticide, a chemical that kills pests. The DDT was sprayed onto crops to kill insects that were eating the crops. It soaked into the soil and was carried by the rain into ponds and streams.

Tiny amounts of DDT entered microscopic plants and animals. Millions of these were eaten by small fish and the amount of DDT in the fish built up. Larger fish ate the small fish. Every time the DDT was passed from one link in the food chain to the next, the amount of DDT became more concentrated. The DDT poisoned a lot of animals as it moved through the food chain.

DDT polluted the rivers and streams. Lots of other things cause pollution and can damage the environment. Here are a few sources of pollution for our rivers, streams, lakes and ponds:

- Rubbish such as plastic bags and bottles carelessly thrown away can harm wildlife.

- Liquid waste, like the treated sewage from houses, is often pumped into local rivers.

- Gases produced by factories and power stations are released from chimney stacks into the air that we breathe.

Figure 1   This landfill site has thousands of tons of rubbish in it.

Figure 2   A sewage treatment works cleans our waste as much as possible, but some sewage still gets into the rivers.

Figure 3   Older, badly kept cars have dirty exhausts. All new cars must have filters in the exhaust to trap some of the poisonous gases.

Figure 4 Factories and power stations produce huge amounts of waste gases.

To try and stop pollution we are asked to **recycle** our rubbish. Many supermarkets have recycling centres where some household rubbish can be sorted into groups. Some of the things that can be recycled are bottles, newspapers, clothes and metal cans.

We do not recycle a lot of the waste that we produce each week. The solid waste that we throw away is taken to large tips and buried in the ground. We call these tips **landfill** sites. As the rotting food and other waste breaks down, they often produce gases. Most of the gas produced is methane. It is poisonous and flammable (can catch alight).

Once a landfill site is full, it can be covered over with soil. After some time the land can be used for building new houses. Builders have to be careful that there is not a build up of gas on the site that could harm anybody living there.

Figure 5 When poisonous chemicals escape by accident into rivers, they can kill many living things, not just the fish.

Questions

1 Why might plastic bags and empty tins be dangerous to animals in the wild if they are thrown away?

2 How did DDT poison large animals?

Questions

3 How many recycling centres do you know about? Make a list of where they are and what can be recycled there.

4 Draw a labelled picture of a recycling centre. Explain how each of the materials will be recycled.

Remember

In your exercise book draw a table with three columns, with the headings 'Liquid pollution', 'Solid pollution', 'Gas pollution'. List all of the types of pollution on this page in the correct column. Then add as many things as you can think of to each column. You might want to work as a small group to do this.

Finishing off!

Remember

Copy and complete the following paragraph using the correct 'p' word from the list.

**protect   people   population
poisonous   prey   predators**

A group of individuals living in the same place is called a _____. The human population lives on the planet Earth. There are over 6 billion _____ living at present, though scientists cannot be sure exactly how many people there are at any one time. In the wild, populations of animals are often controlled by animals that eat other animals. These types of animals are called _____. The animals they eat are called _____. In order to _____ themselves from predators, some animals have found ways of defending themselves. Some animals run faster than the predator, others produce _____ chemicals, others will make themselves look bigger or pretend to have big eyes. Many animals try to blend into the background using camouflage.

Now choose the correct word from each pair and copy the paragraph into your exercise book.

Barn owls feed mainly on **bread/voles**. When there are plenty of voles, the number of owls **increases/decreases** but the number of voles **increases/decreases**. Because the number of voles goes **up/down**, the number of owls will also go **up/down**.

Ecologists will look at pyramids of **number/biomass** to see what is happening to the energy transfer in food chains and webs. A pyramid of **biomass/number** tells ecologists how many of each type of animal there are in a food chain or web.

Question

1   Take a new page in your exercise book. Make a list of all the Key Words from the boxes in this chapter down the side. Take two lines per word. Try to write the meaning of each word without looking.

Then go back and fill in any you did not know or got wrong. Now learn to spell them using the look–say–cover–write method.

Web sites to visit:

World Population Information
   http://www.census.gov/ipc/www/world.html

World POPClock Projection – daily population estimate
   http://www.census.gov/cgi-bin/ipc.popclockw

United Nations Population Fund
   http://www.unfpa.org

Population Action International
   http://www.populationaction.org

CHAPTER 11

Driving the rock cycle

Starter Activity
Natural materials

Stone is a hard, strong natural material. There are many types of stone. In the hardest types of stone the particles are held together very strongly.

a) Some stone is very strong.

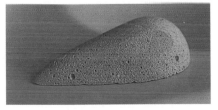

c) Some stone is rough. Pumice is used to remove hard skin.

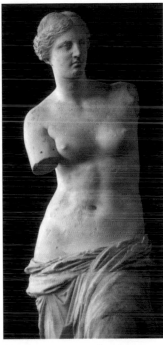

b) Some stone is elegant.

d) Some stone is beautifully coloured.

e) Some stone contains useful raw materials such as metals.

Questions

1 Explain the different arrangements of particles in a solid and a liquid.

2 What is weathering? What does it do to rocks?

3 How does freezing water crack rocks apart?

4 Look at the photos above. Explain why the different types of rock are used for each purpose. Copy and complete the table below. One has been done for you.

5 What can we find out from fossils?

6 What is the difference between a rock and a mineral?

Rock type	Use	Explain its use
granite	castle walls	
marble	statues	
rubies	jewellery	
iron ore	making ore	contains useful raw materials
pumice	removing rough skin	

Solids and liquids in the Earth

Key words

lava   Molten rock on the surface, from a volcano

magma   Molten rock under the surface of the Earth

tectonic plate   A part of the Earth's crust that is in one piece

Making rocks

Most evidence shows that the Earth is 4600 million years old. Its surface has changed a great deal. The surface of the Earth is broken into a number of **tectonic plates**. These plates move about. Mountains rise up as one tectonic plate pushes against another.

1 The centre of our Earth is hot and molten. Only the outer skin of the Earth is solid rock. This solid outer skin is much thinner than you think. Below the skin is hot molten rock called **magma**.

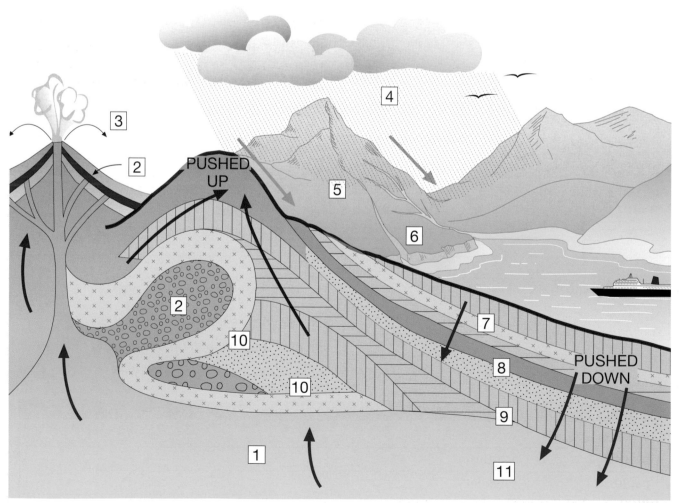

Figure 1 The rock cycle.

Igneous rock

2 As molten rock gets pushed up from the centre of the Earth it cools into solid rock. This is called igneous rock.

3 Volcanoes erupt when the magma pushes all the way to the surface, producing **lava**.

Washing down to the sea

4 Weathering breaks the mountains into smaller rocks. That's why mountains are spiky.

5 Running water in rivers carries away the rocks. As they move they bang together and break up into smaller and smaller bits until they are just sand.

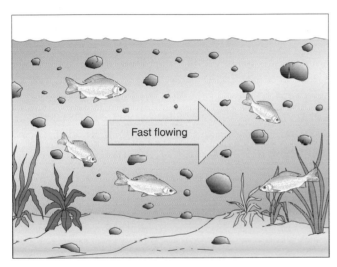

Figure 2 Fast-flowing water carries all sizes of rocks.

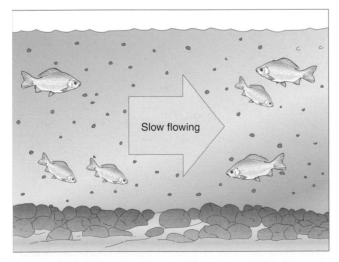

Figure 3 Slow-flowing water only carries small particles of rock.

6 When rivers slow down at the sea, the sand settles out. Sandy beaches are usually found near the mouth of rivers.

Sedimentary rock

7 Over millions of years the layers of sand and mud get thicker and thicker.

8 The layers deep down are squeezed so much that they turn into rock. This is called sedimentary rock.

Heat and pressure

9 The layers of sedimentary rock get heated by the molten magma below them. The squeezing and heating makes the sedimentary rocks change.

10 They change into metamorphic rocks. This big word just means 'changed in shape'. You use a similar word when a caterpillar changes into a butterfly.

Mantle again

11 The rocks get pushed down and down by rocks on top of them. They melt and become part of the magma, and the 'rock cycle' has gone round once.

Questions

1 What makes mountain ranges?

2 What is the centre of the Earth like?

3 How is igneous rock made?

4 What are the rocks made from layers of sand and mud called?

5 What is metamorphic rock?

6 Deep down in the Earth rocks get melted. What is this molten rock called?

Remember

Copy the rock cycle diagram from Figure 1 into your books. Your teacher may give you a photocopy to stick in and label

Making new rocks

Seventy percent of all rocks on the Earth's surface are sedimentary. Making new rock is a very wet process. First, small fragments of sand and rock, called sediment, settle out from slow moving water. This happens where rivers flow into lakes and shallow seas. Gradually over millions of years the layers of sand and rock get thicker and thicker.

The layers of **silt** and stones are squashed together and dry out. Salts and minerals that were in the water are left behind in the rock. These 'glue' the particles together into solid rock.

Figure 2   Different types of cake mix.

Cake is made from flour, sugar, eggs and fat. If you add other things like fruit or coconut, the cake will look different and have a different texture. Limestone is rock made from different minerals, mainly calcium carbonate. But like cakes, not all limestone looks the same. It all depends on what other materials got washed down the river when the limestone formed.

Different? Not really

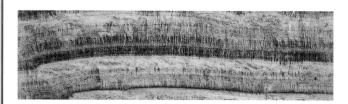

Figure 1   These are all different type of limestone.

Lulworth Cove

Figure 3   You can see the layers of rock or strata here at Lulworth Cove in Dorset.

One hundred and fifty million years ago, Lulworth Cove was once the flat bottom of a quiet sea. The sea dried up and a forest grew on the sediments. Holes can be seen in the stone where the fossilised tree roots once were. Then the forest floor was folded by the same **geological** event that pushed up the Alps to form Europe's main mountain range. The result are these magnificent layers or **strata**.

Fossils

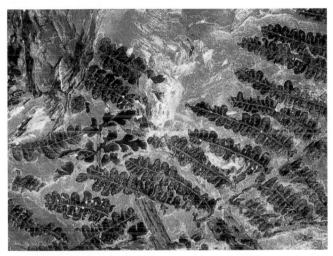

Figure 4 These fossils are of tropical ferns that grew in Germany. The weather must have been very different then.

Figure 5 People put dinosaur skeletons back together from many pieces.

Sedimentary rock is made slowly over millions of years. Deposits of silt are gradually compressed and become solid. It's an ideal place to preserve a record of the past.

Fossils are formed like this:

1 The animal or plant dies and falls into the sediment.
2 The soft parts rot away, leaving just the harder material like bones.
3 Sediments form layers round the harder material.
4 Over a long period of time, the plant or animal remains are replaced by deposits of minerals in the rock.
5 The mineral deposits exactly match the shape of the plant and animal remains.
6 The layers of sediment are eroded away and expose the fossils. The fossils are used to find out what life was like long ago.

Questions

1 Where are sedimentary rocks made?
2 How do the rock particles stick together?
3 Fossils of dinosaurs are not the real bones. What are they?

Remember

Copy and complete the sentences. Use these words:

**millions   sedimentary   fossils
calcium carbonate**

Seventy percent of rocks on the Earth's surface are **s**_____. Limestone is made from **c**_____ **c**_____. Fossils were formed **m**_____ of years ago. We can use **f**_____ to find out what life was like long ago.

Cooking stressed rock

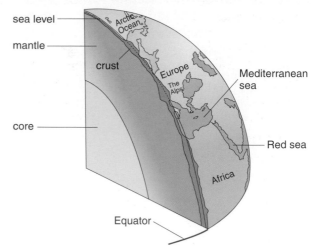

Figure 1   The Earth is not solid. It is like a ball of porridge with a thin crust.

Plate movements

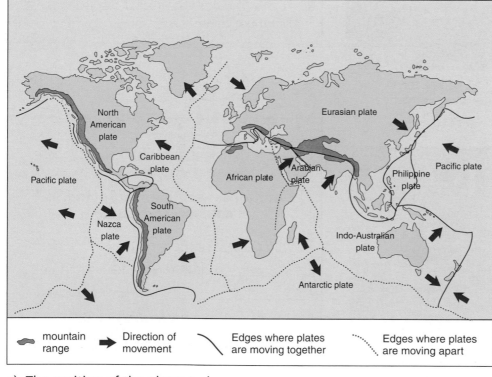

a) The position of the plates today.

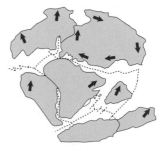

b) The continents as they were 70 million years ago.

c) The continents as they were 140 million years ago.

Figure 2   The surface of the Earth is made of plates that are slowly moving about. The movements cause volcanoes and earthquakes.

The surface of the Earth is not in one piece. It is made of huge areas that fit together called tectonic plates. These plates are slowly moving about. The movements cause volcanoes and earthquakes.

Sedimentary rock keeps on making new rock at the surface. Millions of years go by and the layers of rock get buried deeper and deeper. Metamorphic rock is made when this buried rock gets heated and **compressed**. Pressure comes from the weight of the layers of rocks above pushing down, and heating comes from the molten rock in the **mantle** below.

The rock changes into a new material. This new material is the same colour as the old rock, but it is baked much harder.

Sometimes the magma will force its way up through a weakness in the Earth's **crust**. If it reaches the surface it makes a volcano. But other times it just cooks the material round it to make new metamorphic rock.

Marble and slate

Figure 3 Marble is a very beautiful stone.

Marble is a beautiful smooth stone. It is used a lot for sculpture and fine decoration. Once it was softer limestone, but now it has been baked hard by magma.

Figure 4 A slate roof.

Slate is used for roof tiles. It was once mudstone but the heat has made it much less **porous**.

Marble and slate are both types of metamorphic rock.

Questions

1 What are tectonic plates?

2 What happens when tectonic plates push against each other?

3 How do sedimentary rocks get buried?

4 What heats up the buried rock?

5 Give two examples of metamorphic rock.

Remember

Copy and complete the sentence. Use these words:

heating   hard   pressure

Metamorphic rock is baked **h___** by **h_____** and **p_____**.

Earthquakes and volcanoes

California quake: Seen by a famous writer

Figure 1

The most recent earthquake in the San Francisco region was probably this morning. Small earthquakes happen nearly every day. Every few years a big 'quake' takes place.

Mark Twain and the San Francisco earthquake of 8 October 1865.

Mark Twain, a famous American writer, wrote this passage.

'It was just after noon, on a bright October day. I was coming down Third Street. The only objects moving anywhere were a man in a horse drawn buggy behind me, and a **streetcar** going slowly up the cross street. Otherwise, all was **quiet**.

There was a great rattle and jar in the house I was passing. I thought there was a fight in that house.

There came a terrific **shock**. The ground seemed to roll under me in waves, with a violent joggling up and down. There was a heavy grinding noise as of brick houses rubbing together.

I knew what it was now. . . a third and still worse shock came. I **reeled** about on the pavement trying to keep my footing. The entire front of a tall four-storey building on Third Street sprung outward like a door. It fell across the street, raising a great dust-like volume of smoke!

The streetcar had stopped, the horses were **rearing**. The passengers were pouring out at both ends. One fat man had crashed halfway through a glass window. He was stuck, and was squirming and screaming like a madman.

There was a stream of human beings from every door of every house. As far as the eye could see, there was a mass of people stretching down every street.'

Volcano story

Krakatoa

Key words

dormant   Not active
radiation   Heat from the Sun
scattered   Reflected away
tsunami   Huge wave

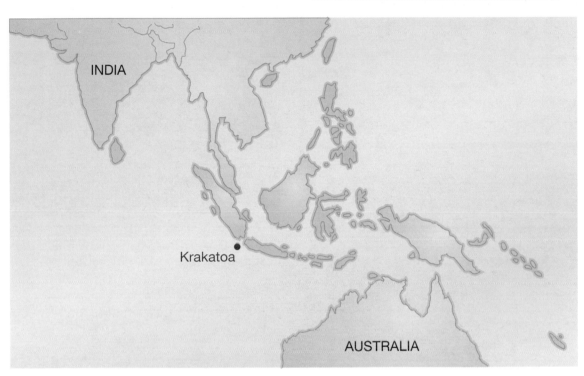

Figure 2

The world's greatest explosion was caused by a volcano. This volcano was Krakatoa, an island in Indonesia.

Krakatoa had been **dormant** for more than 200 years. A **plug** of solid rock had blocked its opening, but unknown to everyone gases were collecting under the plug. One day in August 1883, the pressure of these gases became so great that Krakatoa exploded.

The explosion destroyed two-thirds of the island. It was so loud that it was heard clearly 5000 kilometres away. Rock was thrown 55 kilometres high into the air. Clouds of dust caused darkness for days.

Only a few people were killed by the explosion of Krakatoa. But it rocked the seabed, creating a huge wave. This giant **tsunami** flooded nearby islands. In places the wave was over 35

metres high. It destroyed a total of 163 villages and more than 36 000 people were drowned.

Great clouds of dust from Krakatoa gradually drifted around the world. The dust **scattered** the Sun's rays for the next three years. It caused amazing sunsets everywhere. The dust prevented some of the Sun's **radiation** reaching the Earth, so the world had a series of cool summers and freezing winters.

Questions

1   Draw a picture of what one of these two events must have looked like. You could choose just one scene from the story and draw it.

2   Make a list of the words in **bold** and write their meanings next to them.

Solid rock

Key words

crystal A single grain of a solid

crystallisation When crystals made from a liquid turn into a solid

excited When particles gain energy they move faster

magma Liquid rock underground

texture How rough the rock feels

vibrate The wiggles of particles in a solid

Particles in solids and liquids

Figure 2 Particles in a liquid are like the people in the crowd: they can move about.

Figure 1 Particles in a solid are like the people in the seats. They can only **vibrate** a bit.

The **texture** of rock depends on how quickly it becomes solid.

When liquid **magma** cools down it makes solid rock. The particles become less **excited** and move slower. They link together in regular patterns. Each solid 'piece' that forms from the liquid is a **crystal**. This process is called **crystallisation**.

If the liquid cools slowly it makes big crystals and the rock has a rough texture.

If the liquid rock cools quickly, it makes small crystals. The rock feels smoother. Obsidian is an igneous black rock as smooth as glass. It cooled very quickly.

This effect is seen very clearly in rocks that have been formed from molten magma or lava.

Granite

Figure 3 Granite

Granite rock is formed deep under the Earth's surface. Magma cools slowly to produce large crystals.

Basalt

Figure 4 Basalt

Basalt is a volcanic rock. The lava flows from a volcano and cools very quickly – this makes very small, tightly packed crystals.

Shut your eyes and imagine the dancers in a disco all packed in together. They are dancing in lines with linked arms.

The music gets faster, they move quicker as they become excited. Eventually they dance so fast that they cannot hold on and they break free of each other. The dancers breaking apart is like a solid melting. Crystallisation is the opposite of melting.

Questions

1 Use the 'dancers at a disco' model to show crystallisation.
   a) Draw a picture to show a slow end to the music. The dancers link together again in large groups – like large crystals.
   b) Draw a picture to show a sudden end to the music. The dancers could form lots of very small groups like tiny crystals.

Remember

Copy and complete the sentences. Use these words:

randomly   solids   smooth   quickly

Particles in **s**_____ wiggle about. Particles in liquid move **r**_____.

If a liquid becomes a solid **q**_____, the solid will have a **s**_____ texture.

Brave new island

Some molten magma gets to the surface through cracks in the rocks. This effect produces volcanoes.

In November 1963, fishermen were near the south coast of Iceland. They noticed black smoke rising from the sea.

A plane was sent in to investigate. The pilot confirmed that a new **volcano** had broken through the waves, making the world's youngest island, Surtsey. When the **eruption** happened, ash was thrown 10 000 m into the sky. The birth of Surtsey took almost four years.

There was a lot of **erosion** from the sea. Two smaller islands, that were formed at the same time, disappeared. But the **core** of Surtsey solidified as rock and is here to stay.

The new island is one square mile (2.6 square kilometres) in area and rises 170 metres above sea level, a total of 290 metres from the **sea floor**.

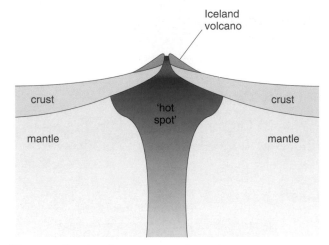

Figure 2   The formation of a volcano.

Surtsey has been carefully watched. It is giving scientists information about how a new island develops, how plants and animals get there and so on. Because the island is so special only a few scientists are allowed to visit it.

Figure 1   An aerial view of Surtsey.

Iceland is part of a chain of underwater mountains that runs down the middle of the Atlantic ocean. It is the place where the North American tectonic plate is pulling away from the European plate. These two parts of the sea floor are moving away from each other. Where the two plates move apart, volcanoes are formed. Iceland has lots of volcanoes. One of the volcanoes is called Hekla. It has erupted 17 times.

Another volcanic island is Hawaii. It is much bigger than Surtsey. The piles of lava that form Hawaii rise as high as 9 750 metres from the sea floor. They have been built up by many eruptions to form the cone-shaped island.

Figure 3 An aerial view of Hawaii, another volcanic island.

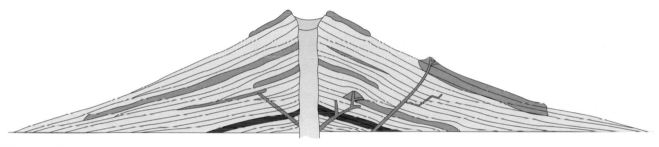

Figure 4 Volcanic islands like Surtsey and Hawaii are built up. Each eruption forms a new layer of rock until a cone-shaped mountain is made.

Questions

1 When did Surtsey first appear?

2 What had created the new island?

3 What happened to the two other islands made at the same time as Surtsey?

4 What is happening on the sea floor to make the volcanoes?

Remember

Copy and complete the sentences. Use these words:

**surface   Europe   Surtsey
lava   volcanoes**

V_____ are formed when molten rock comes out from a crack in the earth's **s**_____. The molten rock is called **l**____ and it cools to make new rock.

The crack that produced **S**_____ island was caused by **E**_____ and North America moving apart.

Finishing off!

Inside the Earth

Mantle: Very hot rock deep below the Earth's surface

Plate tectonics: The movement of the plates of rock on the Earth's surface

Earthquakes: Sudden earth movements caused by plates slipping

Volcanoes: Where molten magma pushes up to the surface

Igneous rock: New rock formed from molten rock

Weathering: Ice, water and wind break up rocks

Transport: When ice, water and wind move rock particles about

Sedimentary rock: New rock made from layers of particles carried by the water

Fossils: Rocks that have formed in the spaces in rock left by dead plants and animals

Strata: Layers of rock, with the oldest at the bottom

Cement The materials that glue sediments together to make new rock

Metamorphic rocks: New rock made by heating and compression

1 Make the words from the list above into a mind map about the rock cycle. Put the word ROCKS in the middle of a big sheet of paper. Write the names of the three main types of rock around it. Draw links and use the other words from the list to show how the different types of rock are made.

Use pictures as well as words. Don't forget to show that one type of rock is made from another.

2 Take a new page in your exercise book. Make a list of all the Key Words from the boxes in this Chapter down the side. Take two lines per word. Try to write the meaning of each word without looking. Then go back and fill in any you did not know or got wrong.

Now learn to spell them by the look–say–cover–write method.

Web sites to visit:

US Geological Survey
http://www.usgs.org

An Applied Science Course
http://minerals.cr.usgs.gov/gips/aii-indx.htm

Sound and music

Starter Activity
Sources and senses

Vibrations travel out from a source of sound. When you speak your voicebox vibrates. You can feel the vibrations if you put your fingers either side of your throat.

MM! MM! MM!

Make a humming sound and feel your voicebox vibrating.

In a cinema, loudspeakers are the sources of sound. The vibrations can travel through the air and through other materials. They make our eardrums vibrate. Special cells in our ears can sense the vibrations.

Many musical instruments have strings which vibrate to make sounds. Others have vibrating columns of air.

The rays of light from a cinema projector travel in straight lines.

Light also travels out from sources. The powerful lamp in a cinema projector is a source of light. We can use 'rays' to show the straight pathways of the light. Sound travels quickly, but light travels much faster.

Questions

1 Name the sources of sound in a cinema?

2 If you listen to live music such as a marching band, what vibrates to create the sound?

3 Put your ear to the desk. Get your partner to rub gently on the desk. Does sound travel better through air or wood?

4 A clap of thunder and a flash of lightning come from the same place. The sound and light start to travel at the same time. You see the lightning before you hear the thunder. Why?

5 Copy and complete this table.

Musical instrument	What vibrates?
guitar	string
trombone	air in a pipe or tube
piano	
trumpet	
drum	
bell	

Travelling vibrations

Key words

eardrum A small sheet of skin or membrane in the ear canal that is made to vibrate by sound

Sounds come from vibrating objects. Usually the vibrations are too fast to see, but if you hold a vibrating tuning fork next to a polystyrene ball, you can see the ball move. If you sprinkle sand on a loudspeaker you can see the vibrations. Sound spreads out from vibrating objects.

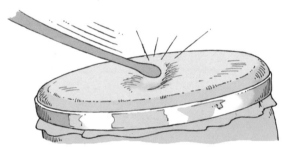

Figure 1 The journey begins at a vibrating drumskin.

The crash of a drumstick makes the drumskin vibrate. You can't see the drumskin vibrate, but if you touch it or put some dried rice on it you might see and feel the vibrations.

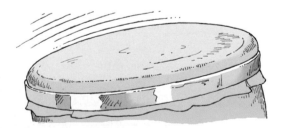

Figure 2 The air around the drumskin vibrates.

The drumskin makes the air around it vibrate. The vibration spreads through the air. The vibrating air makes other things vibrate, but it takes time. The vibrations have to travel through the air. They travel quickly – about one kilometre every three seconds.

Figure 3 Vibrations can travel through all kinds of materials.

The vibrations travel through solid materials even more quickly than they travel through air.

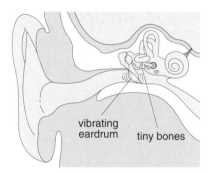

Figure 4 The sound first makes the eardrum vibrate, then tiny bones further in the ear pass the vibrations deeper inside.

The vibrations travel through the air to a small sheet of skin called your **eardrum**. This starts to vibrate too. Your eardrum makes some tiny bones in your ear vibrate.

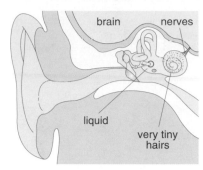

Figure 5 Journey's end – tiny hairs vibrate to make tiny electrical bursts travel along nerves and into your brain.

The bones pass the vibrations on to a liquid deeper inside your ear. There are tiny hairs inside the liquid. They vibrate too. The hairs make tiny electrical bursts in your nerves. Your brain can understand these electrical bursts. Your brain doesn't call them 'vibrations'. It calls them sound.

Loud sounds make you deaf

Loud noises like explosions or very loud music can make the tiny hairs vibrate too much. If this happens they can be damaged. Then they can't make those little electrical bursts in your nerves. Your hearing will be damaged for the rest of your life.

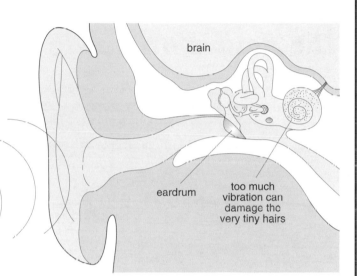

Figure 6 Be careful? Loud sounds can make you deaf.

1 a) What does a drumskin do when you hit it?
b) What does a guitar string do when you pluck it?

2 In what ways is your ear like a drum?

3 Why can it be harmful to listen to very loud music?

Remember

Copy and complete the sentences. Use these words:

**eardrums   loud   vibrating   deaf
air   hairs   brains**

Sounds come from a **v**___ object. The object makes the **a**__ around it vibrate. The vibrations travel through the air. Our ears let us detect vibrations in the air. The vibrations reach our **e**____. Tiny **h**__ deep inside our ears vibrate. The tiny hairs are connected to our **b**___ by nerves. That is how we hear sound. If the sound is very **l**___, the vibrations are very strong. The strong vibrations can damage the tiny hairs. Loud sounds can make us **d**___.

Different sounds

amplitude   The height of a wave. A loud sound has a large amplitude

frequency   The number of waves or vibrations per second

pitch   The frequency of a sound wave. The higher the note, the greater the frequency

The sound of words

You use the voicebox in your throat to speak. When you want to say a word you make your voicebox vibrate. You can make it vibrate in different ways, so that you can make different sounds.

Stop and think!

A Can you feel your tongue move when you speak?

B Can you make loud sounds of some letters just by whispering?

C Try to talk without moving your tongue. Try to talk without moving your tongue *or* your lips.

b) Gentle talk – lungs, voicebox, tongue and lips are all busy. They make louder and quieter sounds. They make high and low notes.

c) Singing out loud – now your voicebox is really working hard. With the help of your brain it carefully makes high notes and low notes. We say the notes have different **pitch**. The voicebox needs to put a lot of energy into vibrations to make loud sound.

a) Quiet sound – you don't need to use your voicebox to whisper.

Figure 1

Sound and music

People all over the world have made many different instruments for making sound. There are hundreds of different kinds of drum alone.

Figure 2 In control of the amplitude and frequency of vibrations.

There are many kinds of string instrument. They all work by making a string vibrate. It takes a lot of practice to make music with strings. You have to be in control of the vibrations.

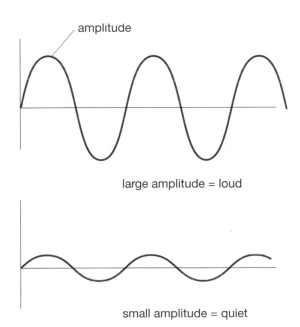

amplitude

large amplitude = loud

small amplitude = quiet

Figure 3 A large amplitude of vibration gives a loud note.

The **amplitude** of vibration is the distance the string moves away from its rest position. When the amplitude of vibration increases, the loudness of the sound increases.

The **frequency** is the number of vibrations the string makes in every second. Guitar strings usually vibrate with high frequency, hundreds of times each second. All you see is a blur. High frequency vibrations make high pitched notes.

Questions

1 Which parts of your body do you use to talk?

2 Which parts of your body have to work extra hard when you sing loudly?

3 The sound made by the strings of a guitar isn't very loud. What does this tell you about the amplitude of its vibrations?

Remember

Copy and complete the sentences. Use these words:

pitch frequency loudness amplitude vibrates

Vibrations of objects make sounds. The amplitude of the vibrations affects the l_____ of the sound. The frequency of the vibration affects the p_____ of the sound. When you talk, your voicebox v_____. You can change the sound of your voice by changing the a_____ and f_____ of the vibrations.

Different notes

> ## Key words
>
> **hertz** The unit of measurement of frequency (Hz)
>
> **oscilloscope** A machine which displays a signal such as that produced by sound waves

Every sound wave carries a pattern. The loudness of a sound depends on the amplitude of the vibrations that caused it. The pitch of a sound depends on the frequency of the vibration.

A microphone is sensitive to sound waves. The sound waves cause vibrations in the microphone. The microphone converts the vibrations into a matching pattern of electric current.

We can use an **oscilloscope** to help us look at this pattern. The oscilloscope is a machine like a TV. It produces a single moving dot on a screen. It turns the electric current from the microphone into patterns that we can see. It makes it easier to compare different sounds. It also makes it easier to work out how frequency and amplitude affect how the sound feels to us.

Figure 1 A singer in action in the recording studio.

Figure 2 A producer in a recording studio can change the loudness of the sound from each instrument.

Music is full of variety. There are bass notes which have a low pitch. They are produced by big bass drums or the long strings of a bass guitar. There are the higher notes of the female singer. They have a high frequency. She can sing them quietly, with low amplitude, or loudly with a large amplitude.

All sound starts off with a vibrating object. The vibrations spread out into the surrounding air. It's a bit like the ripples spreading on a pool of water. The travelling vibrations are called waves.

- The frequency of a sound is a measure of the number of vibrations in every second. It affects the pitch of the note we hear. We measure frequency in **hertz**, or Hz for short. One hertz is one vibration per second.

- The amplitude of a sound is a measure of the size of each vibration. It affects the loudness of the note. In a recording studio, the producer knows how to change and blend the frequency and amplitude to get the best sound.

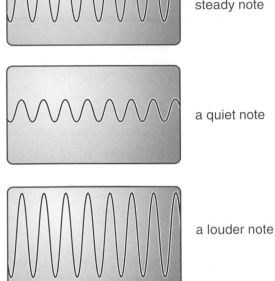

a continuous steady note

a quiet note

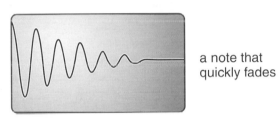

a louder note

a note that quickly fades

Figure 3 Sound shapes as they appear on the screen of an oscilloscope.

1 Which of these notes seen on an oscilloscope
   a) is the loudest to start with
   b) is the highest pitch
   c) dies away most quickly
   d) lasts for a long time?

i) 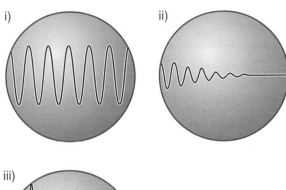   ii)

iii)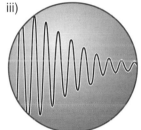

2 Describe the difference you'll hear between these two notes.

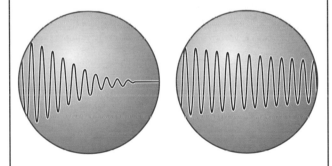

3 Put these words into pairs that go together:

**microphone   amplitude   pitch
frequency   oscilloscope   loudness**

Remember

Copy and complete the sentences. Use these words:

**amplitude   vibrating   waves
frequency   notes**

A song is a mixture of **n___** with varying loudness and pitch. All the sounds are made by **v___** sources such as guitar strings, drumskins and people's voice boxes. The travelling vibrations that spread out are called **w___**. Objects which vibrate with a large **a___** make loud sounds. Female vocalists usually sing notes with higher pitch or **f___** than male vocalists.

Sound travelling and reflecting

Key words

megahertz Unit of frequency.
1 megahertz = 1 million hertz

ultrasound Sound signals beyond the range of human hearing

Sound travels much more slowly than light – almost a million times more slowly in air. The speed of sound in air is about 330 metres per second. But sound can travel through materials that light cannot penetrate.

Figure 1 You hear the tapping sound through the iron railing before you hear it through the air.

Sound travels easier and faster in solids and liquids than it does in gases like air. Its speed in iron is 5000 metres per second. Try tapping a long iron railing. Your friend will hear the sound through the railing before hearing the tapping through the air.

Over a hundred years ago two people measured the speed of sound in Lake Geneva in Switzerland. One made a signal that the other could see and at the same time he struck a bell underwater. The other started his stopwatch and then put his ear under the water until he heard the bell. They worked out that the speed of sound in water is 1500 metres per second.

Silence in space!

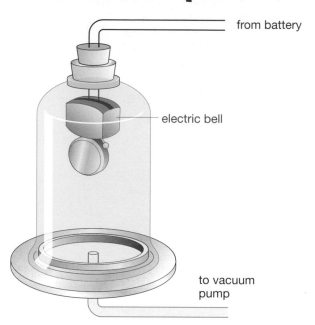

from battery

electric bell

to vacuum pump

Figure 2 The bell is set ringing, but as the air is pumped out of the jar the sound gets quieter and quieter.

Sound travels through air, solids and liquids, but unlike light it cannot travel through a vacuum or empty space. When the air is taken out of a bell jar the sound cannot be heard.

Particles again

Vibrations are the source of all sound. To travel, these vibrations must be passed on – the vibrations of a drumskin must make the surrounding air vibrate. The vibrating air particles must make the air particles next to them vibrate, and so the vibration travels along as a sound wave. The particles in liquids are much closer together and pass the vibrations on much quicker. Sound travels faster in liquids than in gases. In a solid the particles are packed even closer. The vibrations travel even faster.

Reflecting sound

Sound can be reflected. The laws of reflection apply to sound just like they do for light. Reflections of sound are often called echoes. A large, smooth, hard surface like a wall will make a good reflector of sound. An empty room has more echoes than one with carpets, curtains and furniture.

Ultrasound reflections are used to produce images of unborn babies. It is likely that your mother had an ultrasound scan before you were born. Ultrasound is very high frequency sound – too high for humans to hear. The scanner uses a frequency of 3.5 **megahertz**. (3.5 million vibrations a second).

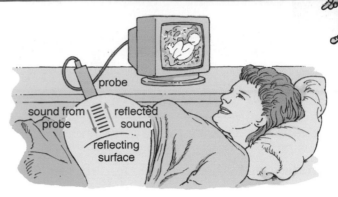

Figure 5 The probe vibrates at a very high frequency to make ultrasound. Then it detects the reflected ultrasound to make a picture of hidden surfaces.

The probe detects the reflections and sends them to a computer which displays them on a screen. It provides a way of checking that the baby is growing as it should.

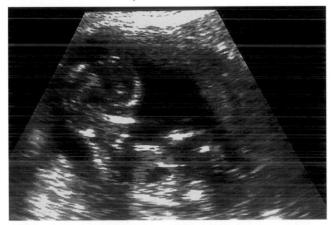

Figure 3 An ultrasound scan of a baby in its mother's womb.

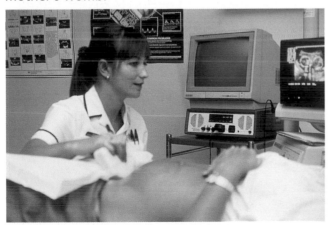

Figure 4 This woman is having an ultrasound scan.

Before you were born, the hospital radiographer will have moved the ultrasound probe across your mother's abdomen (Figure 4). The probe sends out ultrasound which is reflected back from your developing body.

Questions

1 What evidence is there that sound can travel through solids and liquids?

2 **a)** What do we measure in hertz, kilohertz and megahertz?
   b) Copy and complete:

   3.5 megahertz = _____ hertz

Remember

Copy and complete the sentences. Use these words:

**ultrasound   units   high   million
vacuum   metres   faster**

In a vacuum and in air light travels at 300 000 000 **m___** per second. That's almost a million times **f____** than sound. Sound cannot travel through a **v___** but it can travel well through solids and liquids.

An **u___** probe vibrates with a frequency that is too **h___** to hear. One megahertz is a **m___** hertz. Megahertz and hertz are both **u___** of frequency.

Testing hearing

Key words

audible frequency range   The normal range of hearing, usually 20 Hz to 20 kHz

audiologist   A person who tests for hearing

cochlea   Organ inside the ear that is sensitive to vibrations

decibel (dB)   Unit for measuring the loudness of sound

Figure 2   A hearing test will check for deafness.

Frequency range

In your ears, the smallest hairs detect high frequency sounds. They are the easiest to damage. So if your ears are damaged by loud sounds you might not be able to hear high frequency sounds. You could still hear low notes, but be deaf to the high notes.

normal audible frequency range for a young person

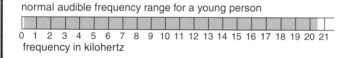

0 1 2 3 4 5 6 7 8 9 10 11 12 13 14 15 16 17 18 19 20 21
frequency in kilohertz

normal audible frequency range for a young person whose hearing has been damaged by loud sounds

0 1 2 3 4 5 6 7 8 9 10 11 12 13 14 15 16 17 18 19 20 21
the worse the damage, the more the audible frequency range is reduced

normal audible frequency range for an older person

0 1 2 3 4 5 6 7 8 9 10 11 12 13 14 15 16 17 18 19 20 21

Figure 1   Some audible frequency ranges.

Children have the biggest **audible frequency range**. As you get older, or if your hearing has been damaged, you cannot hear the high frequencies. You might not be able to hear some of the sounds of speech – especially the high frequency sounds like 'f', 's', and 't'.

To have your hearing checked you will visit an **audiologist**. You will wear a set of headphones and be tested with a range of sounds at different frequencies and amplitude.

The loudness of sounds

We measure the loudness of sound with an instrument called a sound level meter. The loudness is measured in units called **decibels**. A whisper is about 20 decibels (20 dB), normal conversation is 60 dB, a heavy lorry is 90 dB. In Britain the law limits noise levels of 100 dB to only 48 minutes a day. Some personal stereos have dangerous noise levels of 100 dB. Be careful, they could make you go deaf!

Ears – what can go wrong

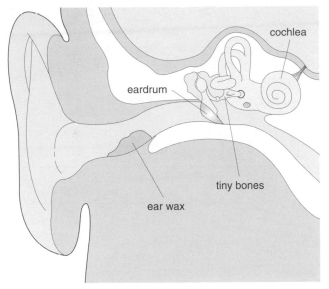

Figure 3 The internal structure of the ear.

- A build-up of wax in the outer ear can cause a temporary reduction in hearing.
- Sound arriving at the eardrum makes it vibrate. The eardrum is a circle of stretched skin. It can be burst by sudden loud noises such as explosions.
- The small bones transmit the vibrations from the eardrum towards the inner ear. They are very small and delicate.
- The **cochlea** is in the inner ear. It is a coiled tube filled with liquid. Small hairs on the cochlea move in time with the incoming sound vibrations. They create electrical signals that travel into the brain. We say that we are hearing sound. The hairs can be easily damaged by loud sounds. There is no way to repair the tiny hairs.

Animal hearing

Animals have different hearing ranges that are adapted to their way of life. We humans can hear from 20 Hz up to 20 kHz, but a dog can hear frequencies up to 30 kHz. They can hear special dog whistles which we can't. Whales make very low frequency sounds which other whales hundreds of miles away can hear.

Figure 4 Bats listen to the echoes reflected off their prey. They can hunt in the dark.

Bats can make very high pitched sounds. They can hear up to 160 kHz. Their squeaks bounce off their prey as echoes. They can hunt for food in the dark.

Questions

1 Loud sounds are a health hazard.
   a) What damage can they do?
   b) In what situations are people exposed to loud sounds?

2 What happens to your audible frequency range as you get older?

Remember

Copy and complete the sentences. Use these words:

**hertz   vibration   kilohertz   decibels
amplitude**

The loudness of a sound depends on the **a**___ of vibration of the sound. It is measured in **d**___. The frequency of a sound depends on the frequency of the **v**___ of the source of the sound. The unit for measuring frequency is the **h**___. Most people can hear sounds in the region of 20 hertz to 20 000 hertz. 20 000 hertz is written as 20 **k**____.

Finishing off!

★ Sound waves spread out from vibrating objects. The travelling vibrations are called waves.

★ Different objects vibrate with different **frequencies** and **amplitudes**. The spreading sound waves then also have different frequencies and amplitudes.

★ If the frequency of the sound wave changes, the **pitch** of the sound we hear changes.

★ If the amplitude of the wave changes, the loudness of the sound we hear changes.

★ Sound waves make our eardrums vibrate. Very loud sounds can damage the tiny hairs in our inner ear.

★ Sound waves need a material to travel through.

★ When ears get older, the ability to hear very high pitched sounds gets worse.

Questions

1 Take a new page in your exercise book. Make a list of all the Key Words from the boxes in this chapter down the side. Take two lines per word. Try to write the meaning of each word without looking. Then go back and fill in any you did not know or got wrong.

Now learn to spell them by the look–say–cover–write method.

2 Name three sources of sound you might hear on a typical day.

3 Read this story: The Sun was shining. The fields looked green and bright except in the dark shadows of the trees. In the distance, Jan could hear the sound of a drum. It was a long way away, but Jan could tell that the drum was being hit very hard. It was a low pitched deep sound. Slowly the sound got louder.
   a) What was the source of light in the story?
   b) Describe the vibrations of the drum.
   c) How did the sound travel from the drum to Jan?
   d) Which travelled faster to Jan, the light or the sound?

4 How can very loud sounds damage your hearing?

5 Look at these signals on an oscilloscope.

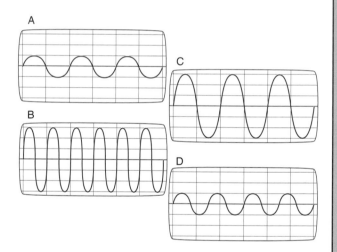

   a) Which sound has the highest pitch? Explain how you can tell.
   b) Which two sounds have the same pitch? Explain how you can tell.
   c) Which two sounds are the loudest? Explain how you know.

Web sites to visit:

Sound website
   http://www.smgaels.org/physics/sound_1.htm

Sense of hearing
   http://tqjunior.thinkquest.org/3750/hear/hear.html

Periodic Table of the elements

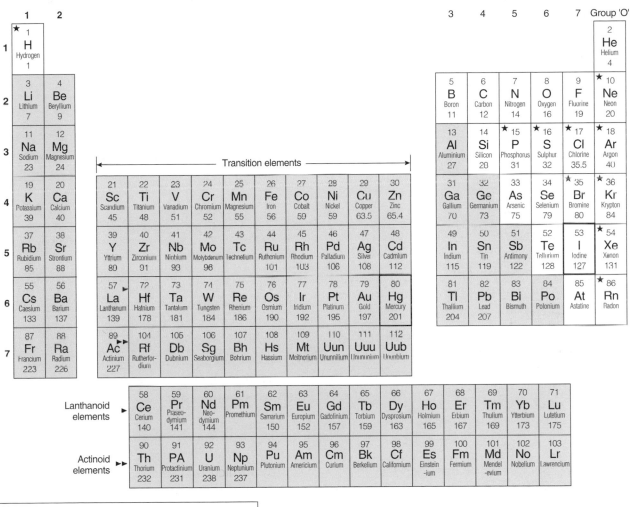

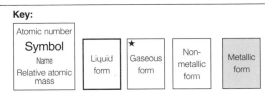

Index

Index